Block for Non IT Professionals

notionpress.com

INDIA · SINGAPORE · MALAYSIA

Notion Press

Old No. 38, New No. 6
McNichols Road, Chetpet
Chennai - 600 031

First Published by Notion Press 2020
Copyright © Srinivas Mahankali 2020
All Rights Reserved.

ISBN 978-1-64869-933-7

This book has been published with all efforts taken to make the material error-free after the consent of the author. However, the author and the publisher do not assume and hereby disclaim any liability to any party for any loss, damage, or disruption caused by errors or omissions, whether such errors or omissions result from negligence, accident, or any other cause.

While every effort has been made to avoid any mistake or omission, this publication is being sold on the condition and understanding that neither the author nor the publishers or printers would be liable in any manner to any person by reason of any mistake or omission in this publication or for any action taken or omitted to be taken or advice rendered or accepted on the basis of this work. For any defect in printing or binding the publishers will be liable only to replace the defective copy by another copy of this work then available.

Block-chain for Non IT Professionals

AN EXAMPLE DRIVEN, METAPHORICAL APPROACH

SRINIVAS MAHANKALI

notionpress.com

INDIA · SINGAPORE · MALAYSIA

INDICACADEMY

Indic Pledge

- *I celebrate our civilisational identity, continuity & legacy in thought, word and deed.*

- *I believe our indigenous thought has solutions for the global challenges of health, happiness, peace, and sustainability.*

- *I shall seek to preserve, protect and promote this heritage in doing so,*
    - *discover, nurture and harness my potential,*
    - *connect, cooperate and collaborate with fellow seekers,*
    - *be inclusive and respectful of diverse opinions.*

About Indic Academy

Indic Academy is a non-traditional 'university' for traditional knowledge. We seek to bring about a global renaissance based on Indic civilizational and indigenous thought. We are pursuing a multidimensional strategy across time, space and cause by establishing centers of excellence, transforming intellectuals and building an ecosystem.

Indic Academy is pleased to support this book.

CONTENTS

Preface — *11*

Acknowledgments — *15*

1. Philosophy of Blockchain — **17**

   1.1 Isn't it all about Ethics? — 17

   1.2 The Importance of Trust — 18

   1.3 How the Trust Is Broken—Fakes All Over — 20

   1.4 The Trust Anchors Ruling the World — 22

   1.5 The Broken Trust—Facebook and Hackers — 24

   1.6 The Way the Transactions are Conducted, Triple Entry Acts — 26

   1.7 What will make you Trust Every Other Person you Deal with? — 27

   1.8 Empowering Peer-to-Peer and Disintermediation — 28

   1.9 Toward a Decentralized World — 29

   1.10 Collective Achievement in Favor of Individual Aggrandizement — 30

1.11	Regaining Trust in Everything We Transact	32
1.12	Towards a World of Sustained Development	34

2. Psychology Behind Blockchain — 36

2.1	We Believe More in Machines than Men	36
2.2	Third Person Provides the Check	40
2.3	Replacing the Vulnerable Third Person with a Machine/Automated Program-Driven System (why?!)	41
2.4	How do you like the Machine to be Permanent, Incorrigible, Fair, Transparent and Democratic?	42
2.5	Decentralization Leads to Faster Decisions. Is it better to depend on one at a Distant Place or a set of Easily Approachable Empowered Decision-Makers Acting in Tandem?	47
2.6	Democracy and Consensus are Better than Autocracy	48
2.7	Distribution Eliminates the Risk of Ransom and keeps the Scamsters at Bay (Ex: Uber, SSOT Newspaper.) Let the Whole World know....	51
2.8	Immutability, Time-stamping, Digital Signature and Auditability can Trap the Errant	52

2.9 If you are going to be found out, better not take a risk and do wrong! Non-repudiation and Accountability Mapping Chain the Participants to Good Behavior	54
2.10 We Love Collective Success Versus Individual's Achievement	55
2.11 Digital Identities and Zero-Knowledge Proofs	57
2.12 Learning from the Aviation Industry	65
3. Promise of Blockchain	**69**
3.1 Book Combines Encryption, Encoding, Hashing, PKI, Timestamps, DSA and Broadcast for the Internet of Value—Privacy, Permission, Passwords	69
3.2 Say No to Fakes	80
3.3 Welcome to a Pure World	82
3.4 Say no to Middlemen—Disintermediation	86
3.5 No More Corruption	87
3.6 Break the back of Cybercriminals	90
3.7 Go for the Goals (SDG)	91
3.8 All the Possibilities to Track	95
3.9 How the ICT-MAAFIAA Can Help	114
3.10 Blockchain 0–10	115

 3.11 Welcome to a World of HOPE   116

 3.12 Companies Consortia and Countries Catalyzing the Blockchain World— Some of the World's Leading Blockchain Consortia are given below   118

4. Projects, Possibilities, Problems   **132**

 4.1 Blockchain-based Application Patterns and Architecture   132

 4.2 Setting and Scaling Up Blockchain Projects   147

 4.3 Deciding on Blockchain Implementation   149

 4.4 Implementing Blockchain—The Six Sigma Perspective   151

 4.5 The Consortium Approach to Implementing Blockchain   154

 4.6 Are you Ready to Start the Blockchain Project?   162

 4.7 Challenges in Implementing Blockchain Solutions   184

 4.8 Roles and Responsibilities for a Blockchain Organization   188

Annexure: A-To-Z of Blockchain Ecosystem   *193*

PREFACE

If there is one Magical Technology that can excite everyone with its amazing potential, utility and benefits for mankind, galvanizing a whole new generation of digital futuristic professionals, it is 'Blockchain.' The last 5 years have seen a rapid change in the understanding of and approach toward Blockchain, the new technological paradigm that has hit the world.

There were two occasions (2014 and 2017) in my life when I was critically ill and almost on the verge of death. The struggle for survival on these occasions has led me to the discovery of many new paradigms I did not focus on, before. One of them is Blockchain. As I lay on the bed for months during these two stints, I learned more and more about Blockchain and Cryptoassets and developed an urge to not only explore these technologies more and more but also to explain them clearly to the entire world and put them in the right perspective! This led me to conduct Training and Corporate workshops while consulting on many projects. I wrote *Blockchain, the Untold Story* in 2018 which was translated to Chinese within three months of its launch and also put me in touch with many brilliant professionals,

It is now clear to almost anyone that Blockchain not only offers a solution to the many risks being faced by an increasingly centralized and digital world but also is catalyzing refreshing changes in the way we work and respond to events.

In this book, we shall delve into the different dimensions of Blockchain as depicted in the following figure:

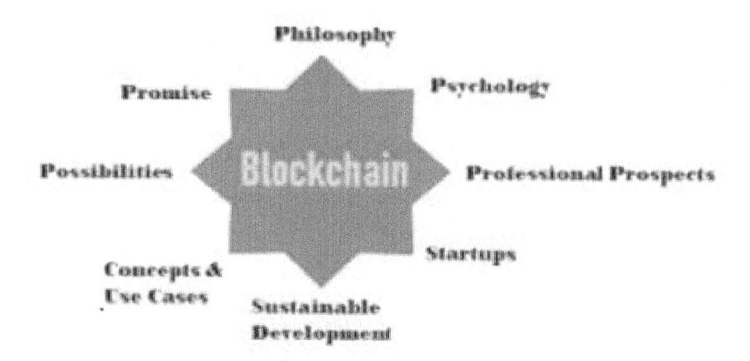

Philosophy, Psychology, Professional Prospects, Startups, Sustainable Development, Concepts & Use Cases, Possibilities, Promise — Blockchain

Dimensions of Blockchain explored in this book

A democratic, decentralized, distributed, programmable, tamper-evident and immutable ledger can help Start-ups from innumerable compliance tracking issues and empower them to collaborate for collective success. Efforts to achieve the United Nations' Sustainable Development Goals can get a big boost with the help of Blockchain.

Collective achievement over individual success, a democratic approach based on consensus instead of an autocratic approach and co-operative-style working instead of working in isolation to the extent of even collaborating with the competition, have been facilitated by the

Blockchain machine and this is being celebrated by many progressive-thinking persons.

By acting as a Trusted Third Party in a programmatic manner, Blockchain is bringing in unforeseen trusted interactions, eliminating non-value adding middlemen. This is leading to increased efficiencies and affordability, lowering costs and a vastly improved environment that offers pure, genuine and authentic interactions, products, services and information for customer delight.

Blockchain offers these possibilities by abstracting several technology paradigms that are hitherto simple in nature, by combining them beautifully.

While it was always within the reach of technology professionals to understand and engage with this amazing paradigm, it was necessary for people in all walks of life too, to understand and leverage this paradigm, which is not just a combination of technologies, but also to explore and pursue the immense possibilities

Though there has been no dearth of learning material around this topic, a majority of the interested persons are still unable to grasp the exact reason for its popularity and also the essence behind this paradigm that endears itself to all who come anywhere near it.

This work aims to demystify Blockchain's many dimensions and make the reader appreciate all the concepts behind this amazing technology paradigm in a simple and engaging manner.

The reader is expected to understand various facets and utility of Blockchain and also be able to clearly visualize opportunities to implement in every potential opportunity.

The enterprises and many Governments across the world are finding new use cases of Blockchain every day and it is only a matter of a few more years for us to be totally used to patronizing any service or product that is able to demonstrate its authenticity and purity, an essential feature of a Blockchain solution.

Starting from each and every individual concept that is required to plan for the launch of an appropriate Blockchain use case, this book aims to clear the confusion that one has about the approach to leverage Blockchain for the right use case in an informed manner.

The book covers most of the common concepts required to understand Blockchain in a simple manner in the first three chapters. However, in the fourth chapter, we step up the gear to cater to those who want to delve more into the technology and understand its architecture and implementation in more detail. This will enable you to gain some amount of mastery over the subject and support your knowledge needs in managing a routine Blockchain career as well. This can also plan to explore your career options with the utmost clarity.

For those who are interested in a Technical or a Developer role, there are many resources available in the form of books, white papers, On-line and Off-line short-term and Post Graduate courses that can train and arm you with the skills and expertise required to become a successful professional.

Hope this book will prove to be a great resource to understand and appreciate this enigmatic but Magical Technology paradigm. Welcome to the ***Blockchain Religion.***

ACKNOWLEDGMENTS

My works as the employee of the most respected Industry (NASSCOM) and Government-owned Organization like NISG, COE lead at Kerala's most respected organization, ULCCS group and Program Director at India's first and leading Amity University's online Blockchain Post Graduate certification program and as the author of one of the World's highest-rated Blockchain books (with over 85 ratings on Amazon) have offered me a great opportunity to immerse in the work in my favorite paradigm called Blockchain which combines aspects from many domains including Technology and Business Management.

I got an invaluable opportunity to interact with many leading technology companies and customers for Blockchain that helped me understand the technology expectations and possibilities.

I am thankful to Sri. Manish Jain, CEO, BPB publications, who initiated my journey as an author and to Mr. Jayavel Sundaravinayagam, CEO, JPA Solutions, Chennai for discovering my training skills.

I came across professionals like Srishty Jain, (Founder, CoLLearn), and Santosh Ganesh, who wanted to educate different types of learners like Teenage Children, Micro, Small and Medium entrepreneurs in whose hands the future of this world is taking shape.

I am also fortunate to be aided in this effort by many brilliant youngsters, one of them being Krishna Swaroop, Kozhikode, Kerala, a Computer Science graduate from Amrita University, Coimbatore who always amazed me with his passion for cutting-edge technologies and his ability to learn them quickly to be able to also help me in formulating my thoughts on complex concepts into simple explanations.

This is the outcome of many such inspirations, experiences and insights gathered along the way.

I would like to sincerely thank all those who inspired me and supported me in pursuing my journey in Blockchain. I sincerely thank Mohammed Naquib, Head of Technology at IBF Net for his review and suggestions to improve the content.

Thanks to Sri. JRK Rao IAS, CEO, NISG, and Ms. Debjani Ghosh, President NASSCOM, for continuously and passionately pushing us for emerging technology adoption.

Mr. TN Hari, Head-HR, Big Basket, Ms. Shradha Sharma, Founder, YourStory Media, Mr. Manish Jain, CEO, BPB, Dr. Raghavendra Prasad, CEO, Astra Quark, Raveendran Kasturi, CEO, ULCCS, Mr. Ajit Chauhan, Chairman, Amity Future Academy, my senior colleagues at NISG, M.V. Ramana Sir and others and Blockchain leaders, entrepreneurs and gurus, inspire me to contribute my best at my job and to society.

Above all, I wish to thank my family members with special emphasis on my wife Anuradha and Father-in-law, Sri. V.S.R. Murthy, a brilliant banking and finance professional, who acted as a sounding board to me to crystallize some of my thoughts to be able to put in a language understandable to non-technology professionals.

Thank you.

1

PHILOSOPHY OF BLOCKCHAIN

1.1 Isn't it all about Ethics?

Ethics is the very essence of a righteous human life.

There was a time in this world when there was no fear of any thief or anyone cheating another.

People used to say that the traders used to leave their shops with valuables open and were not afraid that someone would steal them. That was ages ago.

As time progressed, the values and morals took a back seat to the attainment of a comfortable and cushy life. The focus shifted on to the attainment of 'Short-term goals' and to undertake 'Shortcuts' to achieve one's end, no matter how.

Even the most trusted Governments have at times, had to overlook the corrupt practices of the scamsters, without any morals, out there to corrupt the society we live in.

Fig 1.1 Fake Certificates, Forged Signatures, Adulterated Milk.

What do you do when you can't depend on the ethical behavior of those you interact with, depend on or undertake transactions? What happens if you cannot 'Trust' anyone else?

1.2 The Importance of Trust

"Trust" is the cornerstone for all interactions we have between different entities, human or otherwise. We interact freely with those we trust. We listen to those we trust with an open mind. We buy things we trust and from those we trust. In fact, when we deal with someone we trust, we do not need any middlemen. Isn't it so?

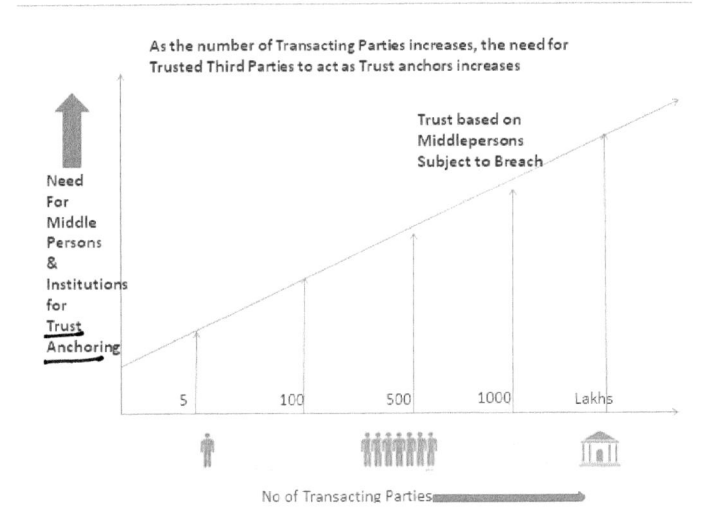

Fig 1.2 Trust deteriorates with scale.

But it is the same trust; that is often broken by the same we trusted.

As our circle interactions grow and organizations get bigger leading to more and more transactions, we end up trusting a variety of middlemen, whether it is Governments, banks, large organizations or leaders in different businesses. The more we trust them, the more of our values we offer. Where we don't have people, we depend on institutions and structures like contracts or agreements to save us through courts of law. These are called the 'Trust Anchors' also referred sometimes as 'TTPs or Trusted Third Parties.' Trust Anchors extract a lot of value from us for this service and very often disproportionately.

1.3 How the Trust is Broken—Fakes All Over

You plan to buy some automobile spares and you come across an enticing ad.

Can you trust the claims of the jazzy ads that rule the e-commerce world with heavy discounts or for that matter even the brick-and-mortar giants that entice you into their stores with never-before offers?

This may be a very genuine advertisement. But would you trust and buy from any small and unknown vendor? Or, do you pay a premium and rather buy from a 'Trusted' site like 'Amazon'?

Is there any mechanism or a platform that is well-known and trusted by many?

What is the root cause of all these?

There is a whole new breed of entities that is ever waiting to take advantage of this phenomenon: the phenomenon of masquerading, counterfeiting, adulterating or 'Faking.'

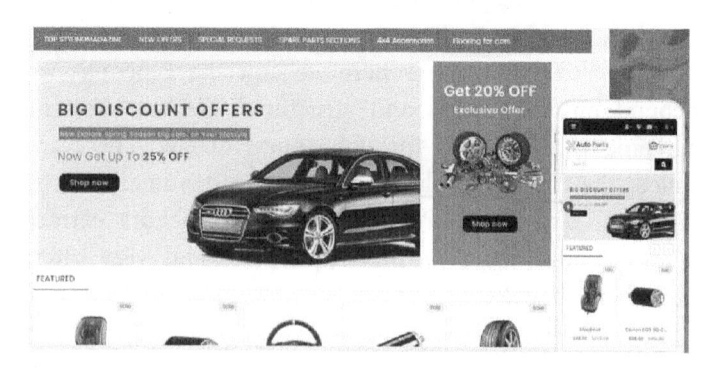

Fig 1.3 Commonly-faced Claims by middlemen in our daily lives—Can you trust?

How sure are you that the medicine you are buying is not a 'Fake' drug?

How sure are you that the imported 'Sunglass' you are buying is indeed imported?

The foreign 'chocolate' you are buying is indeed made in the country.

We Are Facing Trust Deficit In Every Sphere Today

- Fake Identities & Rampant corruption
- Fake Identities Inflated Benefit Claims
- Subsidies & benefits
- Medicines
- Defective, Spoilt, Spurious Food Adulterated milk
- Certificates, licenses & credentials
- Manipulating Voting By Robbing Identities
- Faking Death claims & Wrong Insurance Claims

- Blockchain makes possible tamper proof and secured
- Identification mechanism of users and people; and
- Accounting and record maintenance of the transactions to curb compromise of schemes introduced by Co-operatives

Do your due diligence while shopping online: Third of ecommerce buyers get fake products

Notice issued By UIDAI To 'Illegal' Aadhaar Card Holders

The Unique Identification Authority of India (UIDAI) which issues Aadhaar (12 digit unique number) has issued notice to illegal holders. UIDAI's Hyderabad office on Tuesday sent notices to 127 people for allegedly obtaining Aadhaar numbers on 'false pretenses'.

Fig 1.4 Fakes all over.

The same with any precious metal or the certificate of your employees too! The list is endless!

What is the reason for so many 'Fakes' in our day-to-day life?

Does it have to do with the diminishing standards of 'Ethics' in the world we live in?

This leads to the requirement of the '<u>Verifiability</u>' of the very 'Trust' which is deemed to be above verification itself!

1.4 The Trust Anchors Ruling the World

The ICT-MAAFIAA

Over time, we have begun to depend on very large entities that have captured our imagination and the markets they operate in and have become the facilitators of peer-to-peer transactions across the world through their channel, thus becoming the de-facto we depend upon in all facets of our lives.

The way transactions are conducted today can be depicted in a simple manner in the following diagram.

Interactions in a Centralised System

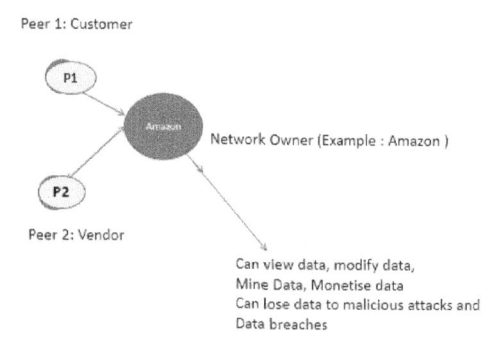

Fig 1.5 Interactions in a Centralized System.

Open your mobile phone and you will find many such 'Trust Anchors' that act like the 'Transaction Brokers' that offer a huge convenience to all their clients, nevertheless!

Fig 1.6 We Blindly Trust these anchors.

I – Intel
C- Cisco
T- Tesla
M- Microsoft
A- Alphabet
A- Amazon
F- Facebook
I- IBM
A- Apple
A- Alibaba

In other words, the giants that can be described by the acronym—ICT-MAAFIAA are the real rulers of the world we live in, in many ways.

In many ways, we end up depending on these companies globally for most of our online transactions and value transfer. Can we say we have become the prisoners of these centralized organizations?

Fig 1.7 ICT MAAFIAA.

1.5 The Broken Trust—Facebook and Hackers

The trust in the so-called 'TTP' started waning in the recent past owing to several events that are shaking the world like data breaches, cyber-attacks and rampant use of data mining activities to influence their customers and monetize the information in unforeseen ways.

The Most Expensive Cyberattacks

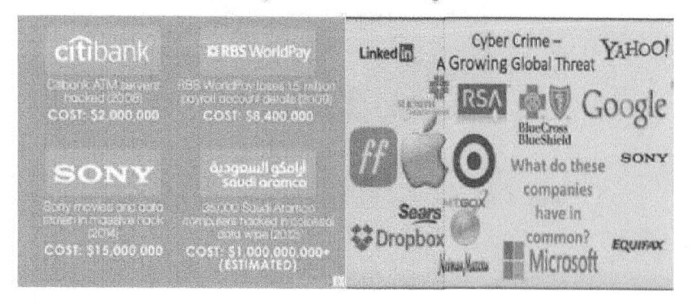

Most admired Global leaders and the best in their business, but continuously pursued by malicious cybercriminals leading to loss of humongous losses at times.

Fig 1.8 The Most Expensive Cyber-attacks.

Most of the organizations we see today operate with a centralized command and control approach and pose meaty targets for the cybercriminals and the ill-minded technology hackers to pursue their goal of compromising the security of the good-willed and the value mines and hold them to ransom

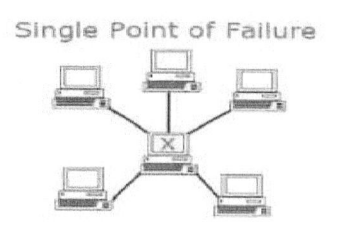

Fig 1.9 Single Point of Failure

Single points of failure.

for their personal gains in unethical ways. In other words, the systems of today are characterized by 'Single Points of Failure.'

The DDOS attack in October 2016, where over a hundred thousand of IOT devices were compromised and accessed by a cybercriminal to flood the top global sites with unauthorized traffic leading to their shut down, the case of Cambridge Analytica, siphoning out valuable personal details to apparently try and influence US elections' outcome and several other attacks on the leading global organizations opened the eyes of the world citizens to the increasing risk posed by the mammoth growth of centralized organizations and to their customers.

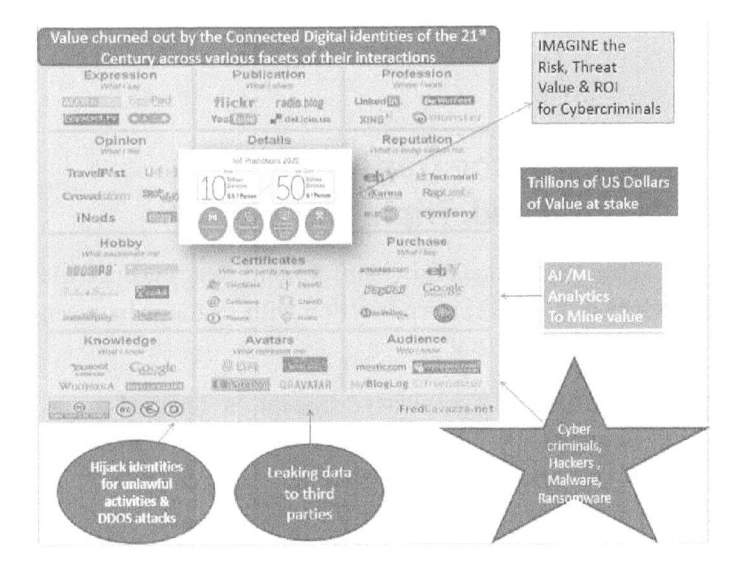

Fig 1.10

WEF has repeatedly ranked the threat of data breaches and cyber-attacks in the top five risks faced by humanity. With the increased digitization the value of the data is also growing exponentially and the world is looking for a solution to de-risk this automation-led growth.

Imagine what would happen if the billions of connections that are continuously transacting on the net and generating voluminous and valuable data are compromised through multiple sophisticated attacks by the cyber criminals!

> "All Programs in the future will be written in a way that there is no 'Single Point of Failure.' There is no one Server that can die and take down the service"
>
> – Ray Ozzie

1.6 The Way the Transactions are Conducted, Triple Entry Acts

'Trust but Verify,' said Sir (Late) Ronald Reagan, once the President of the USA, in connection with relations between his country and Russia!

The Trusted Third Party concept is referred to as Triple entry-accounting for the financial and value transfer transactions. Can this be extended to all aspects of our interactions and offer the security for 'peer-to-peer' unknown entity interactions across the world? We will come to that later.

The importance of the 'Third Party' and can you depend on it all the time? Most of the mishaps in human interactions happen due to misplaced trust.

> "The Blockchain does one thing: It replaces third-party trust with mathematical proof that something happened."
>
> – Adam Draper

Let us take the case of the 'Online Cab Hire Platform' passengers who were attacked by their drivers. There was a time when women passengers were very scared of traveling by the Online Cab Hire Platform taxis. That is when the GPS-tracking of the cars for every route was introduced that could be monitored by the platform. This surveillance by the third party has given the 'Trust' for the vulnerable passengers to travel fearlessly at any time of the day. This is also very much like the monitored CCTV cameras that put a check on the miscreants in public places or protect vulnerable properties.

1.7 What will make you Trust Every Other Person you Deal with?

But what happens when this trust is misplaced, and the third party is political or corrupted?

The tamperable evidence in case of any issue was not serving its real purpose.

The evidence was then shared to every party to the transaction that could be tracked on a live basis. Only then it presented a sort of a foolproof solution that served its end leading to 'nil' of such nature. But there are still problems with this 'centralized' approach of marketplace platforms. That of the 'data breaches,' 'data privacy violation and misuse' arising out of the 'centralized nature' of the Platform administration that could also act as a Single Point of Failure (SPOF).

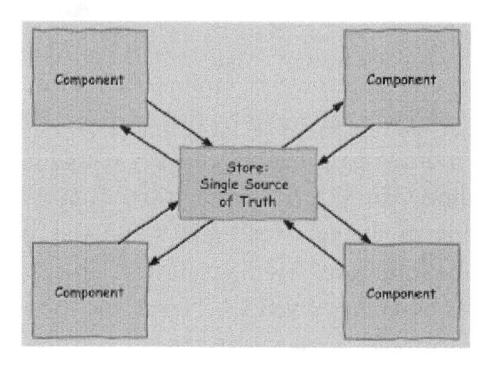

Fig 1.11 SSOT – Sharing of same data from the source between all peers.

The Single Source of Truth offered by the sharing of information across several parties simultaneously has the potential to keep the scamsters at bay and reduce the propensity to fraud.

1.8 Empowering Peer-to-Peer and Disintermediation

Empowering the Small Guy to offer the 'Trust' of an established player and Disintermediation.

Imagine a world in which the small businessman is able to offer the same level of Trust as the established 'Trust' anchors.

Imagine a world in which you can carry out a trusted transaction with any other entity in the world without the worry of their 'Trust' level.

Imagine a world that offers a level playing field between a small business and the largest businesses.

Imagine a world, where you do not have to worry about the data breaches and Ransomware attacks.

Imagine a world in which you can safely and securely hold your personal identity-related information and can monetize it.

Imagine a world where you are sure about the origin and provenance of what you buy and can believe the credential presented to you.

Imagine a world, where we can minimize the amount paid to the Trust Anchors who also pose several other risks discussed earlier.

All these look like a Utopia from the lens of the times we are living in and the challenges we face. Let us see how Blockchain, the new Technology and Business paradigm offers a possibility to realize the above imagination.

1.9 Toward a Decentralized World

'Centralization' always has inherent problems associated with it: that of 'Single Point of Failure.'

Centralization offers a pointed target to the attacker and often, it gives way. Whether it is the 'King' protected heavily inside a fort, or the 'life' of Ravana, the mythical demon king, preserved securely in his belly, history is replete with examples of the plots that could finally succeed in overpowering the 'centralized' targets. The Single Point of Failure posed by the centralized approach has other downsides too. It compromises the speed of decision-making, very often comprising the most precious of the resources while also suffering from the multi-layered approach-related costs and associated vulnerabilities.

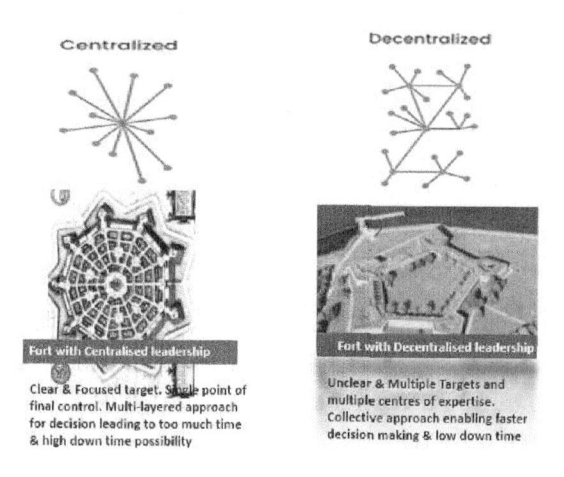

Fig 1.12 Centralized Versus Decentralized Forts.

The advantages of a decentralized/federated governance approach are now well understood and accepted leading to a movement toward decentralization, devolution and delegation of decision-making powers that drastically empower the participants while increasing uptime.

1.10 Collective Achievement in Favor of Individual Aggrandizement

We live in a world that places undue importance on 'Material Success' as an end than on the 'Means' to achieve glory. Individuals/small groups of persons are always on the pursuit of their personal success and to prove themselves to the rest of the world.

The 21st century so far has seen the rise and fall of many individuals or person-driven entities that have courted phenomenal financial success and are revered as the icons of the century. Many such individuals have also strived hard to uplift their employees and the society around them through charitable acts and by searching for their personal success in the success of the society around them.

The evolution of the materialistic society with an increasing focus on short-term achievements sometimes leading to deprivation of ethics is leading to the risk of several individuals corrupting those in power, gaming the system and misplacing the trust to gain phenomenal heights. Some of these get caught by the law and the press and are shown their place, while most of them go scot-free till their end.

> "Happiness is not in the mere possession of money; it lies in the joy of achievement, in the thrill of creative effort."
>
> – Franklin D. Roosevelt

There also have been cases where the founding members undertake a democratic approach and collective prosperity-driven culture where the stakeholders are made partners in progress.

The world is now getting more tuned to recognizing such icons who are sacrificing their individual pursuits for a better and prosperous society.

The recent case of some of the most admired promoters of the century like Bill Gates, Jeff Bezos, Azim Premji, etc. devoting a majority of their property for the enhancement of the living standards of the deprived and also to achieve Sustainable Development Goals of the planet is a strong indicator to this trend.

Blockchain, as a platform that facilitates this collective approach through a decentralized process of decision-making and a transparent reward system that operates like a co-operative, is now being seen as the greatest tool for achieving and rewarding a collective brilliance than an individual-centric effort.

> "Talent wins games, but teamwork and intelligence win championships."
>
> – Michael Jordan

Further, a cohesive, collaborative, co-operative and coordinated approach through a platform that facilitates perfect communication among the participants has the potential to bring out far better results than the efforts of a few smart individuals working in secrecy for solving the world's problems.

1.11 Regaining Trust in Everything We Transact

Can you insure against the third-party risk?

As we can see, the key to undertaking transactions that involve an exchange of any value is to have a mechanism of safeguarding against the counterparty risk. This leads to the search for a 'Trusted' middle party that mitigates the trust and guarantees the transacting parties of potential frauds and criminal behavior ending up in exposure to unwarranted risks.

What if there is a platform that offers a mechanism to mitigate and minimize this risk allowing peers anywhere in the world to transact with any other counterparty without the need for a Trusted Third Party?

Can the platform act as an insurer of the risk that arises between transactions between two peers who are hitherto unknown to each other even before, irrespective of their size?

In the game between a small guy (David) and a big guy (Goliath), can the small guy have his due and equal chance to win, commensurate with his capability?

Will this lead to a balance of power between the Davids and the Goliaths of the business world? Can the world's leading organizations comprising the ICT-MAAFIAA play a part in creating these platforms? Will the availability of such platforms lead to a re-balancing of power between the various actors in the business world and lead to a paradigm shift? Will this tilt the power back into the hands of the individual customers offering them a choice as well as the ability to monetize their personal value, thus realizing the goal of the internet of achieving an empowered global citizen?

> "The internet went from a democratizing free space to having power very centralized; crypto-decentralization is a reaction to that."
>
> – Elizabeth Stark, Co-founder, Lighting Labs

Well, the paradigm of Blockchain seems to be having the ability to achieve many of these goals with the active support and participation of the same forces that have led to the concentrated digital hotspots. How it does, is what we can see in the coming chapters.

1.12 Towards a World of Sustained Development

The growth of population by over five-fold in the past century has resulted in an enormous strain on the environment. The increased industrial activity and need for natural resources, has led a rapid depletion, while the demand is on the surge on the other hand. Hence there is a global movement toward adopting Sustainable Development practices by the countries across the world led by the United Nations Organization, leading to the announcement of 17 goals (SDG https://sustainabledevelopment.un.org/) to be achieved by all countries in this regard by 2030. These will also help in minimizing the contamination and pollution we are faced with across all walks of our life and Blockchain can be a great aid in achieving these too!

SPOF, double-spending, central authorities, middlemen, multiple versions of the truth, inability to pinpoint the problem-creator and reward the righteous: all add up to the 'contamination.'

The philosophy behind the Blockchain is to lead the world toward 'Equality,' 'Democracy,' 'Collective thinking and Collaboration,' a world that offers a counterparty risk-mitigating mechanism to ward against the unethical behavior that surrounds all around us and fill the world with trust and ensuring provenance and authenticity of every product and service we consume.

By steering clear of the single points of failure, offering a single source of truth to the transacting parties and also a foolproof mechanism to ensure creation and distribution of the value over the internet, Blockchain aims to sidestep the need of Trusted Third Parties aka middlemen, thus slaying layers of inefficiency that plague us in many ways negatively.

By offering a transparent, immutable, auditable and durable record of transactions, Blockchain offers to act like a watchdog that fixes accountability for any malicious and crooked activities that play havoc in our day-to-day lives.

The world is gripped with the need to achieve Sustainable Development Goals as laid down by the United Nations, to be achieved by 2030, that could let us pass on an inhabitable planet to our progeny and Blockchain offers to be the records keeper, rewarding mechanism, guide and a watchdog to keep the countries and enterprises on track to progress toward the goal…

> "The Old question – 'Is it in the database?' will be replaced by 'Is it on the Blockchain?'"
>
> – William Mougyar

There could well be a time, in the not too distant future, when the whole world swears by the words, '**In Blockchain, we Trust.**'

2

PSYCHOLOGY BEHIND BLOCKCHAIN

Be Decent in front of the World

2.1 We Believe More in Machines than Men

Let us start with a book

All of us would have read many books. It is easy for us to understand when we relate anything complex to a printed book.

A printed book has a fixed number of pages carefully curated by the editorial team in consultation with the author. The copy is available in the hands of several readers who purchased them.

Assume you want to change the contents of the book and eliminate some pages. For this, you need to first be able to convince the editorial team to agree for the change and then update the book with the revised content and put it up for sale to all the new buyers. It is virtually impossible to change the content in the existing set of books already in the market. If you change the content of the books in your hand by tearing off some pages, it does not reflect the actual contents in any way.

Assume that the pages in each book represent the ledger containing the fingerprint of the transactions undertaken by a set of people whose details are being tracked on the ledger.

Each line contains a transaction converted into a unique evenly sized fingerprint and is linked to the previous transactions appearing in the preceding line through a time-stamp and each page is numbered in sequence.

We now have a ledger of transactions conducted between peers in the system, verified and taken on record by a group of people and then distributed to all the members. This record is then virtually not tamperable.

For this book, we now have a few interesting possibilities:

The book could be accessed by anyone and the opportunity to suggest and vote on changes could be with anyone like in Wikipedia.

The book could be accessed by anyone, but only a select team of editors and authors can review and commit the changes.

The book could be a classified document like an internal training manual given to a select few inside a company for a selective in circulation and created by an exclusive team of people within the organization.

The book could be a classified document for an open circulation to all the subscribers only, but the creators and maintainers are an exclusive club of authorized persons.

We can now try and see the similarities between the 'Book' and the Blockchain approach.

- Blockchain creates an immutable ledger of transaction records that are decided upon by a set of people,

- The result is then distributed to a variety of people who can access it as per any of the four scenarios above,

- Any change in the ledger records needs to be once again created, approved, committed and distributed offering a new record of events,

- The different types of scenarios described here are termed respectively as

   i. Public Permissionless

   ii. Public Permissioned

   iii. Private Permissionless

   iv. Private Permissioned

Guess what would have happened if instead of all the decision-making team members and the members accessing the ledger, only one ledger is kept to keep track by a central party, say a Bank and the rest do not have any rights or access to propose modifications? This is called **'Centralization'** and suffers from **Single Point of Failure** and a **'Single Source of Distortable Truth'**! Very similar to Centralized Databases governed by the Central Authorities!

Blockchain, on the other hand, introduces us to different paradigms from what we are normally used to in our day-to-day life.

Decentralized ledger: Instead of a central authority/admin having data, multiple parties could take part in the decision-making process and have proof of transaction.

Imagine an exclusive Whatsapp group with only one admin having the authority to add new members to the group versus a Whatsapp group that has multiple admins with power to add new members. If one wants to become a part of the exclusive group and take part in the valuable communication in the group, they need to approach one of the many administrators to get added to the group. This vastly improves the continuity, scalability and speed of growth of the membership and also adds to the vibrancy of the communication. The administrators can have a process of voting among themselves upon the requests from the new entrants. This is the process of consensus that allows multiple parties to safeguard the interests of the group to keep off unwanted entrants, rather than depend on the whims and fancies or limitations of a sole group-administrator or the decision-maker. This example explains the process of decentralization at multiple levels in a system, which is one of the processes that characterize most of the Blockchain applications.

Distributed/shared database: The data is stored and updated simultaneously in multiple locations as per the access controls built-in and business requirements.

We are always used to the concept of 'Redundancy' of IT infrastructure that is provided for, in the form of multiple replicated databases or identical nodes, that offers the resilience to the systems in case of failure of the primary systems. As against 'Redundancy' that is undertaken under a single administrator/owner's control, 'Distribution/Sharing' provides for the replication of the information across multiple parties thus providing for resiliency many times over with diminished probability of simultaneous failure/corruption/contamination.

Double-spending protection: The system ensures that the transactions are not repeated and violating any records leading to wrong/overspending or unauthorized activity.

Broadcasting the proof of transaction to multiple parties on a live basis as and when they happen does the job of virtual tamper-proofing leading to an almost immutable record while the distributed database takes the game away from the fraudsters by eliminating the 'Single Point of Failure' as now the data can be recreated from other members of the group who share the ledger. Recording an immutable verified data offers the 'Single Source of Truth' to all concerned.

The system has another benefit. The proof of a transaction between any two members (say peers) in the system is carried in the records of several other members in the system in an immutable manner with evidence of any tampering also to be recorded with due approvals!

2.2 Third Person Provides the Check

Does it not remind one of the 'Triple entry' accounting that we are always used to? It is only that the 'Trusted Third Party' is a group of members carrying the chronologically ordered and time-stamped blocks of the Blockchain system!

The entire world runs on the Triple entry-accounting where the Trusted Third Party offers the safety net to the parties undertaking transactions. The Trusted Third Party can be an

Amazon—For the vendors and customers on the e-commerce platform,

Government—For the notarized agreements,

Banking system—For two persons undertaking financial transfers between their accounts.

The Trusted Third Parties are ruling this world, as we have seen earlier. Most of the time, they extract disproportionate value while sometimes even failing to provide the Trust that is required when their systems get hacked or data gets breached by unlawful actors or when they use the information in unapproved ways!

The search is on for an incorruptible TTP that works like a machine through a transparent program that can never fall short of your expectations. Blockchain has the potential to become such a system, as the world is coming to discover!

2.3 Replacing the Vulnerable Third Person with a Machine/Automated Program-Driven System (why?!)

But hang on. Human beings are always suspicious of services rendered by other humans because of several reasons ranging from corruption to being routinely error-prone or for acting under the undue influence of interested parties.

What if this 'TTP' service is offered by a 'Black Box' like a machine or a set of machines operating in tandem through tested and agreed-upon programs running smoothly? What if you have the business logic and the contractual agreements between transacting parties, encoded in the form of computer applications also known as 'Smart Contracts' that can be triggered to execute automatically upon conditions being met without manual intervention or subjective interpretation?

A Smart Contract is a computer protocol intended to digitally facilitate, verify, or enforce the negotiation or performance of a contract. Smart Contracts allow the performance of credible transactions without third parties. These transactions are trackable and irreversible. (Wikipedia)

Isn't there a trend toward believing and trusting 'Machines' more than 'Humans'?!

The below quote by one of the finest Technology evangelists, Ian Khan sums up the value, a system like Blockchain can provide!

> "As revolutionary as it sounds, Blockchain truly is a mechanism to bring everyone to the highest degree of accountability. No more missed transactions, human or machine errors, or even an exchange that was not done with the consent of the parties involved. Above anything else, the most critical area where Blockchain helps is to guarantee the validity of a transaction by recording it not only on the main register but a connected distributed system of registers, all of which are connected through a secure validation mechanism."
>
> —Ian Khan, TEDx Speaker | Author | Technology Futurist

2.4 How do you like the Machine to be Permanent, Incorrigible, Fair, Transparent and Democratic?

Over the years, the cost of infrastructure in the form of storage space and processing power required for IT applications has come down substantially. The availability of high-quality Cloud service providers has reduced the need for investments in high-cost on-premise infrastructure. Approaches like 'Open-source technologies,' decentralized methodologies and 'Pay-as-you-go-for-services-consumed' are combining to facilitate the employment of cutting-edge technology powered infrastructure to find new solutions to our problems, rather cheaply. Messaging Protocols, Event-driven communication and record updation, API (Application Programming Interfaces) are facilitating collaboration between applications across multiple on-Premise and Cloud-based applications acting together seamlessly. IBM, Microsoft, Oracle, Amazon and many leading organizations are offering high-end secure IT applications including Blockchain as a service that can facilitate the large-scale implementation of automation enabling technologies in a convenient and cost-effective manner.

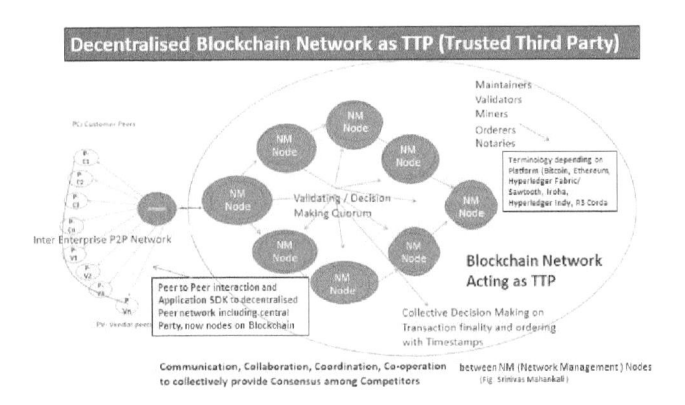

Fig 2.1 Decentralized Blockchain Network as TTP (Trusted Third Party)

Resilient Data Structures of Blockchain

We have seen that in the traditional approach, the participants in a typical business scenario pretty much operate in silos and all the parties are connected to the centralized big market place or the dominant player who connects the buyers and sellers or provides the services to the clients globally.

Instead, Blockchain presents an inter-enterprise scenario where all the peers are connected to every other peer with a possibility to conduct peer-to-peer transactions as per business logic codified in the form of Smart Contracts. Even the dominant player, though while being the facilitator could still be a player whose returns depend on the quantity and quality of the business dealing happening on the network.

We can see the transition that is taking place in the data structures as we shift from traditional centralized databases in the conventional systems to the futuristic Blockchain data structures as summarized below:

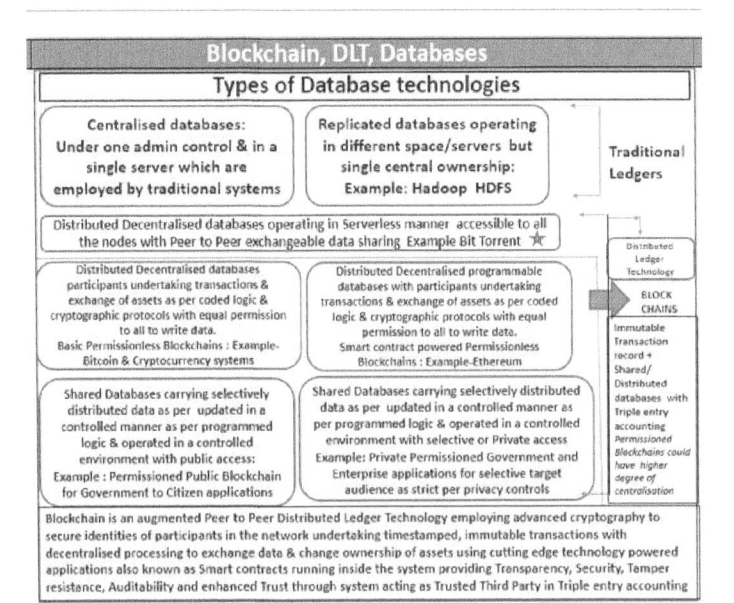

Blockchain, DLT, Databases
Types of Database technologies

Centralised databases: Under one admin control & in a single server which are employed by traditional systems	Replicated databases operating in different space/servers but single central ownership: Example: Hadoop HDFS	Traditional Ledgers
Distributed Decentralised databases operating in Serverless manner accessible to all the nodes with Peer to Peer exchangeable data sharing Example Bit Torrent		Distributed Ledger Technology
Distributed Decentralised databases participants undertaking transactions & exchange of assets as per coded logic & cryptographic protocols with equal permission to all to write data. Basic Permissionless Blockchains : Example- Bitcoin & Cryptocurrency systems	Distributed Decentralised programmable databases with participants undertaking transactions & exchange of assets as per coded logic & cryptographic protocols with equal permission to all to write data. Smart contract powered Permissionless Blockchains : Example-Ethereum	BLOCK CHAINS Immutable Transaction record + Shared/ Distributed databases with Triple entry accounting Permissioned Blockchains could have higher degree of centralisation
Shared Databases carrying selectively distributed data as per updated in a controlled manner as per programmed logic & operated in a controlled environment with public access: Example : Permissioned Public Blockchain for Government to Citizen applications	Shared Databases carrying selectively distributed data as per updated in a controlled manner as per programmed logic & operated in a controlled environment with selective or Private access Example: Private Permissioned Government and Enterprise applications for selective target audience as strict per privacy controls	

Blockchain is an augmented Peer to Peer Distributed Ledger Technology employing advanced cryptography to secure identities of participants in the network undertaking timestamped, immutable transactions with decentralised processing to exchange data & change ownership of assets using cutting edge technology powered applications also known as Smart contracts running inside the system providing Transparency, Security, Tamper resistance, Auditability and enhanced Trust through system acting as Trusted Third Party in Triple entry accounting

- BitTorent is older generation of DLT with distributed hash tables & double spending and is not exactly considered to feature a Ledger

Table 2.1 Databases, Distributed Ledgers and Blockchains.

But, then who is guaranteeing the sanctity of the transactions and providing the trust needed for the conduct of the transactions, which was hitherto being provided by the dominant centralized player, for example, 'Amazon' in the case of the Amazon e-commerce market place? The trust is provided by the Blockchain network that acts like a black box of which all the transaction participants are a part of their Blockchain network-specific identities provided by the administrator.

It is very important, however, to note here that the credibility and financial soundness of the 'Founding group' who are part of the administration group should have a demonstrated credential and credibility to offer a long-lasting platform for times to come. The role of the Governments here to authorize, recognize and regulate such entities cannot be underestimated. Otherwise, the platform promoters should have demonstrated credentials like the 'Big 4' consortia of any business or that of the United Nations!

Very often the Blockchain network, though operating like an independent entity, is promoted by the dominant player who adopts a leading Blockchain platform and joins forces with a major technology player and an infrastructure provider at times.

Some examples that can be sited are, IBM, Walmart-promoted Food Trust, IBM-Maersk promoted TradeLens, Honeywell-Boeing promoted GoDirect Trade, ITD Income Tax department, India—Infosys-promoted tax information network in India—and the like.

What are the returns for the Blockchain infrastructure provider?

The users of the platform have a lot to gain in the form of increased efficiencies, better services provided to their customers and a drastic reduction in third party risk, increased cybersecurity and resilience and reduction in operational costs owing to digitization. For this, they will pay a fee to the administrating organization of the Blockchain platform as per an agreed pay-per-usage model thus resulting in a win-win scenario.

In the case of Permissionless Blockchains like Bitcoin and Ethereum, heavy costs are incurred by the maintainers of the consensus mechanism who offer the TTP benefits to the participants. For this, the miners are rewarded by a combination of currency minted by the network and the transaction fees paid by the participants.

While in the case of Enterprise Blockchains the participants' identities are fully disclosed and verified for compliance with the regulatory authorities, in the case of Permissionless Blockchains, there is a real possibility of ill-intentioned and malicious participants to take over the network or push illegal transactions leading to 'Double-spending.' While this is a routine issue with smaller sized Permissionless platforms, in the case of large platforms like Bitcoin and Ethereum, the network pushes the miners to spend a high amount of resources like computer processing power and electricity to validate their transactions. This leads to a negative ROI (Return on Investment) for malicious participants making it non-remunerative to attack the system.

However, the fall-out of this is that the Permissionless Blockchain platforms consume disproportionately high resources that could one day pose a threat to environmental sustainability.

There is an increasing tendency to innovate on different types of resource-efficient consensus algorithms for use by Permissionless Blockchain platforms (example: DPOS, Tendermint, Proof of Stake, Proof of Elapsed Time, etc.), which could be explored in detail by technically minded professionals.

2.5 Decentralization Leads to Faster Decisions. Is it better to depend on one at a Distant Place or a set of Easily Approachable Empowered Decision-Makers Acting in Tandem?

The important feature of this Blockchain approach is the 'decentralized' approach where the decision regarding the correctness of the transactions is taken without recourse to an individual entity's authority and muscle power. The transactions with due approvals and authorizations representing the real-life scenario are sent to a pool of network managers, who can then collectively follow a designated approach and vote on the transactions to be included in the approved chain of events that influence the records and ledgers permanently.

The decentralized pool of miners is referred to under different names in different Blockchain systems and serves to increase the uptime of the network manifold while minimizing the risk associated with a centralized approach. While in Permissionless Blockchains we have mining pools or set of validators, on Permissioned Blockchains for enterprise applications, they operate as a set of Orderers (Hyperledger Fabric), Notaries (R3 Corda), Validators (Hyperledger Sawtooth, Indy) and the like.

Though these networks start with single such nodes in the beginning, in multi-enterprise scenarios, they operate in a pool (also with replication for Disaster Recovery purpose) and follow appropriate consensus mechanisms depending on the requirement by the administrators of the network.

The network offers 'Decentralization' at different levels. The network effect of combining multiple transacting parties into one channel creates a technically decentralized system for pushing the transactions through a client and the validation and ordering of these transactions is undertaken in a decentralized manner by the Blockchain infrastructure.

2.6 Democracy and Consensus are Better than Autocracy

India, UK and the USA are some of the greatest examples of democratically run countries.

The people of these countries exercise their will and vote for those who form the governing councils to formulate the decisions. Every major decision that affects the people of these countries is put to voting across multiple layers of the political and administrative infrastructure before being put for execution. For example, the key bills that encapsulate the Government's decisions are debated for their impact and property and put to vote in Lok Sabha and Rajya Sabha that house the elected/nominated representatives of the people of the country.

It is a well-known fact that democracy unlike autocracy or a single party rule offers many advantages and also empowers the subjects.

Blockchain offers an amazing feature that empowers the participants to collectively communicate, coordinate and co-operate with each other to make decisions about the transactions that are put through to the network and recorded permanently. This process is called the 'Consensus' mechanism and is considered the heart of the system.

Blockchain involves distributed computing and multi-agent systems and uses processes to agree on output values in relation to various inputs needed during the computation in a reliable manner even in the presence of several faulty processes. This process is called the Consensus process that results in decisions like, whether to commit a transaction to a database, agreeing on the identity of a leader, state machine replication and atomic broadcasts.

Bitcoin protocol that was launched on January 3rd, 2009, the first known application of the Blockchain technology paradigm, reliably provided a solution for achieving such a consensus in distributed systems that create and transact value over the internet without fear of 'Double-spending.'

This problem was formulated into a story called 'Byzantine General's Problem' where a group of nine generals decided to attack a fort they were surrounding, subject to the majority's decision despite being handicapped by improper communication facilities. A 25-year wait after the problem's formulation, Bitcoin successfully demonstrated a solution for the computer systems to achieve Byzantine tolerance even in the face of a sizable number of adversaries and adverse conditions.

There are different types of consensus mechanisms like POW (Proof-of-Work), POS (Proof of Stake), DPOS (Delegated Proof of Stake), PoET (Proof of Elapsed time), PBFT (Proof of Byzantine Tolerance), RBFT, RAFT, N2N and many more. A detailed discussion on these various consensus mechanisms is out of the scope of this manuscript and several white papers are available for understanding and evaluating the same.

One may refer to this article on Consensus mechanisms by KPM.G at https://assets.kpmg/content/dam/kpmg/pdf/2016/06/kpmg-Blockchain-consensus-mechanism.pdf

---

An interesting discussion on Design patterns for Decentralization can be looked up at https://www.youtube.com/watch?v=JDrdgk1L-ww (Design Patterns for Decentralized Protocols Avoiding Blockchain)

– Daniel Hardman

2.7 Distribution Eliminates the Risk of Ransom and keeps the Scamsters at Bay (Ex: Uber, SSOT Newspaper.) Let the whole World know....

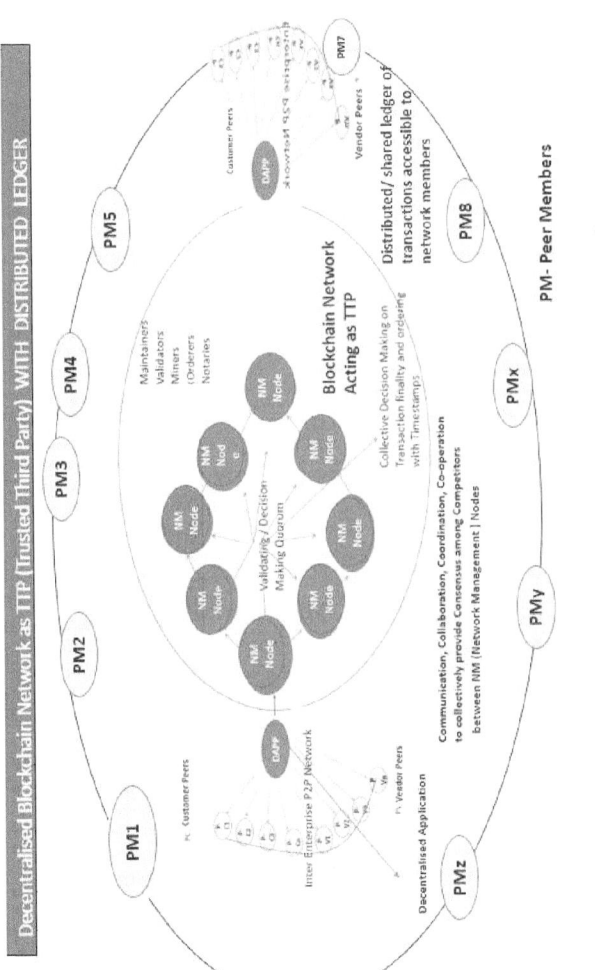

Fig 2.2 Distributed, Decentralized Blockchain Network as TTP (Trusted Third Party)

The Single Point of Failure has always been the bane of most of the centralized organizations which maintain their databases under a single command, control and administration. This is the weakness most often exploited by the Ransomware virus creators who were behind some of the most lethal attacks on global organizations by unleashing the WannaCry virus.

While Distribution and shared database also help in non-repudiation by the parties undertaking transaction, the ability to reconstruct the database from other members of the network eliminates the risk of the SPOF from the very route thus blunting the weapons of the cybercriminals. This minimizes the risk by tilting the RRR (Risk-Reward-Ratio) away from the investors in these crooked instruments.

Thus, Blockchain is seen as the vehicle for safe and secure automation at scale.

2.8 Immutability, Time-stamping, Digital Signature and Auditability can Trap the Errant

The Blockchain records are considered immutable and highly tamper-resistant. Every approved transaction is time-stamped and recorded in the STR (Sender Transaction Receiver) format.

Every transaction is identified by the sender's digital signature and there is no possibility of repudiating the responsibility pertaining to that any time ever. The intended receiver can unlock the contents of the transaction with the sender's digital signature with the help of his secret (private) keys and there is only a limited chance for any middleperson to access the contents. Once the transaction is broadcasted and distributed in a block and added to the Blockchain, there is little one can do to alter it even in the future.

We are used to databases that are managed by centralized administrators and governed by central authorities in the system. The traditional database technologies follow the 'CRUD' (Create, Read, Update and Delete) methodology of updating the datasets embedded inside their tables or graphs. This gives a scope for data mutation that can alter the data at the will of the miscreants and wrong admins, leading to mistrust and fear of modifications.

In contrast, we have seen that the records on Blockchain's data once appended can only be changed by subsequent correction entries and not by altering any information present on the ledger. This improbability to change the data on Blockchain ledger helps in preserving the 'data integrity' with a possibility of verification or auditability of the appended information at any point in subsequent times.

In case anyone undertakes a willful misdeed or presents a wrong certification, this event will be permanently recorded and will come into light one day or the other.

This immutability and auditability are critical differentiators with respect to the traditional database approach. Further, the Blockchain databases are also programmable using Smart Contracts and can update the transactions in response to real-life events, unlike the static databases we are used to.

This feature allows us to track the changes in ownership of assets or manage permissions and access in fields like Supply chain management, Land records, Tokenized assets, etc.

2.9 If you are going to be found out, better not take a risk and do wrong! Non-repudiation and Accountability Mapping Chain the Participants to Good Behavior

Blockchain, as we have seen, uses a combination of activities like Identity Management, Decentralized decision-making, Serverless architecture, Distributed ledger, etc., to record the events and transactions that ensures transparency, accountability, auditability and immutability.

For this, various elements of the distributed architecture are used like smart contracts-powered programmable database technologies, processing and computation, replication, messaging, event recording and updating and many more. An interesting discussion on different architectural aspects and patterns used in distributed database systems can be seen at https://www.youtube.com/watch?v=tpspO9K28PM (Four Distributed Systems Architectural Patterns by Tim Berglund)

While in Permissionless Blockchains that use pseudo identities, it becomes difficult to identify the participants in case they have participated in any illegal transfers or stealing value units, in Permissioned Blockchains, implementation and adherence to excellent KYC/AML regulations and management of authorized member identities through accredited MSP (Membership Service Providers) ensures that any mistakes done in the system could be identified easily and attributed to the member's real identity easily.

Once recorded with a time-stamp, since it is impossible to delete the record, in case of the propensity to undertake any illegal and irresponsible transactions, the system will be able to trace the events to the precise event recorded and the identify responsibility for the same.

This ensures that virtually no one dares to take a risk and commit any misdeed or wrongful and malicious activities on the system. This is like a CCTV camera installed in a premise that not only continuously records and tracks the event, but also ensures that the data can never be altered or deleted.

This property of the Blockchain entails it to be a great candidate for many applications that track the provenance of things, drugs, vegetables, digital records and also puts a check on the usage of 'Fake' identification, certificates and the like.

2.10 We Love Collective Success Versus Individual's Achievement

By nature, the Blockchain approach changes the dynamics of interactions from a centralized approach to a decentralized approach.

Also, the individuals will be empowered to protect their identities with the help of DID and DKMS based systems (Decentralized ID management and Decentralized Key management systems) in such a way that they can selectively disclose their identities and various parameters of the same to requesting parties and possibly monetize their value as well.

Organizations like Sovrn, Evernym, Uport, SecureKey are specializing in providing Decentralized Identity management systems already being implemented by countries like Canada, Belgium, Switzerland (Key cities) and the like.

Disparate Centralised Systems to Networked Decentralised Systems

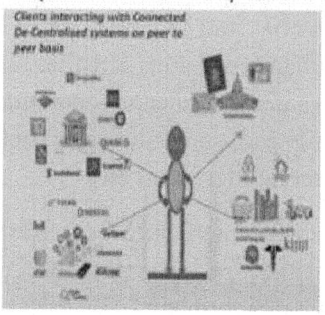

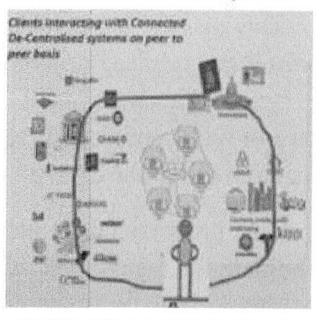

Current Approaches   Blockchained world Approaches

Fig 2.3 Disparate Centralized Systems to Networked Decentralized Systems.

This brings to fore another important point. The Blockchain-based approaches call for protection of privacy of the participants, collective approach to running organizations and managing them with utmost accountability and sharing the returns rather than solely monetize the traffic through advertisement and unlock value by selected promoter individuals or groups.

This approach allows for a more equitable distribution of wealth and we will see many prosperous entrepreneurs collaborating for providing accountable growth to their clients through decentralized applications and enhanced productivity engineered processes.

The organizations can also benefit by a collective pooling of the addressable target market that can also make up for some of the losses arising out of the decentralized approaches limiting their ability to monetize their customer base in the current manner.

2.11 Digital Identities and Zero-Knowledge Proofs

Identities and digital signatures for Access, Authentication and Authorization are the critical components of a Blockchain paradigm that provide the critical 'Security,' 'Privacy' and 'Confidentiality' to the participants in the network.

The Identity Management of citizens is a very important facet of the individual's rights. However, the multiplicity of interactions and the potential unauthorized use of personal information in an indiscriminate manner for commercial purposes open a Pandora's box of ethical issues along with personal security concerns. Blockchain offers a unique Digital Identity Management system that offers the safety and security of their personal data and allows the members to provide permissions to users of the identity information. The concept of self-sovereign identity and decentralized key management system offered by platforms like Hyperledger Fabric, Hyperledger Indy or Uport enables the organizations to register members uniquely over a Public Permissioned network.

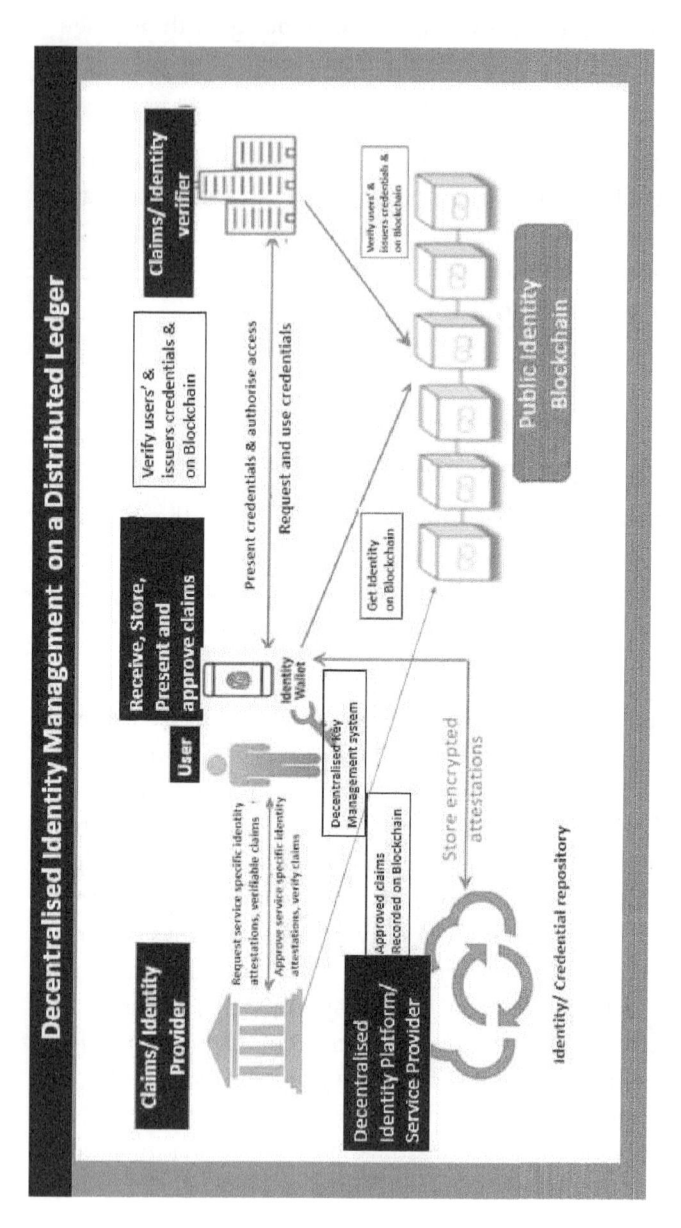

Fig: 2.4 Blockchain-based Self-sovereign Identity with Decentralized IDs and Decentralized Key Management system.

Case Study: Decentralized Identity Management and eKYC (Source: Aurigraph DLT)

The Aurigraph DLT proposed a Decentralized Identity Management on Distributed Ledger Technologies to deliver enhanced digital citizen services while ensuring joint control of citizen and business data and User-controlled Privacy and Data Security. Government, Businesses and citizens should be able to access data and services across the distributed ecosystem and data sources for transparency and non-repudiation. The Government and its various departments will be able to access data over Aurigraph DLT platform while being able to track and trace data and transactions from heterogeneous platforms in one infrastructure.

The National DLT backbone would offer a seamless platform for verified Citizen, Business and Government interactions that would be shared on a public ledger while maintaining requisite privacy.

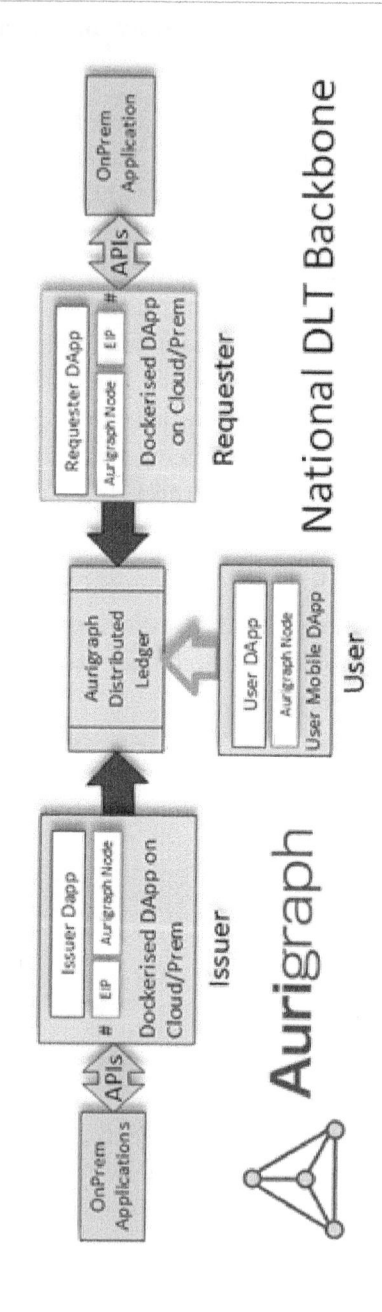

Fig 2.5 Aurigraph Decentralized Identity platform.

Issuer

A document or data issuer is the source of the records. An Issuer DApp (Decentralized Application) will be integrated with the issuer systems to handle requested data with requisite authentication using Aurigraph Enterprise Node using REST APIs and Web Services. The issuer will respond with digitally signed data linked to a QR code to service the request which would be recorded on the Aurigraph public ledger. The ledger record would include the Issuer-certified data along with necessary digital identification.

Requester

A Requester may request an Issuer-certified document from an issuer through the approval by the affected Citizen using a DApp with Aurigraph Basic or Enterprise node. A Requester will place a request to the concerned citizen or business for document(s). Upon receiving the approval from the citizen or business entity, the request is forwarded to the issuer who may then release the requested document with appropriate permissions to the Requester. The Requester can use the document for the requested purposes only and any further shares will be only after the user's approval with an update on the public ledger. The Requester may access the data using the QR code as well.

User

A citizen or business may provide necessary identification to the register using a self-signed sovereign identity with biometric authentication and request issuers for the relevant records and documents which will be stored in the citizen/business' Digilocker (Store of all personal credentials on a Government's centralized platform) vault on the user device. The documents issued to the user are valid for use only by the user and can be controlled using user-defined permissions.

User Services

User Services may draw citizen or business records and documents from respective issuing departments and businesses using appropriate authentication and share the same with requesting parties with due authorization. The data records will be drawn from multiple departments to be secured in the citizen's Digilocker vault on the user's device using decentralized identity management.

The user may view the list of services and documents on his device running a Mobile User DApp with Aurigraph Node. The User DApp will participate in the consensus as well. The user may give his approvals for data and document requests on the user DApp. All user interactions such as approvals will be recorded on the public ledger for immutability and transparency. The User may store all his records and documents in his Digilocker vault in his device with the option to back up the vault on a Cloud.

Business Services

Business Services may include Business registration with supporting documents such as ID proof, address proof, and other collateral. The same may be used to request multiple services from various department and agencies for licensing, tax and Bank account and other applications. Further on, Credit checks and tax returns can be initiated through the same DApp leading to reconciliation and settlement of accounts along with Bank and tax reconciliation. Businesses can use the same platform for other functions such as license applications, employee background checks, compliance reporting, credit check and loan applications. Government notifications may also be delivered on the same system.

Government Services

The Government may offer a suite of digital services to Businesses and citizens. These could include processing applications and petitions directly handling and delivery. The Government may choose to deliver notifications and alerts directly to businesses and citizens with a digital auditable trail, delivery confirmation and read receipt that may be linked to Smart Contract for follow-up action.

The Government services could also include tracking of criminal activities and records from all departments and security agencies as a centralized database would be impossible to maintain.

Governments may also conduct elections and surveys at a fraction of cost and infrastructure used today while ensuring the integrity of the data collected and its immutability. The results would be reported immediately after closing hours with the count being taken in real-time.

Use Cases involve collaboration among users, businesses and Government for delivery and consumption of services. The Roadmap starts with decentralized identification infrastructure, authenticating citizens and business and aggregating their respective documents from the issuers in the users' Digilocker account. Users can issue and consume documents and services securely from the same Digilocker as a service. Examples include:

1. Citizen Identity Management across decentralized and heterogeneous sources

2. Land records, Building plan approvals, tax assessments and payments and the consequent bank reconciliation

3. Permits and Licenses

4. KYC processing for citizens and business entities

5. Employee background verifications

6. Employee payments with salary, income tax, provident fund and professional tax reconciliation

7. GST reconciliation across a value chain for input tax credit

DBT Track-and Trace under Central and State sponsored schemes to beneficiary

Zero-Knowledge Proofs allow the members to selectively disclose their identity without revealing confidential information. For example, the ZKP system allows the member to prove that he/she is above 18 years without the help of a Pan card or reveal his/her Bank balance is above Rs 10000/- without revealing the actual account details that could be confidential information.

Estonia, considered one of the most digitally advanced countries, has put in place a comprehensive digital identity verification platform for its nation's citizens, where citizens identified through their access card with identities registered on a Blockchain can access any of the Government and most private services and provide conditional access to their credentials that identify them without disclosing too many private details. The citizens' identity is used by the Government and private sector to provide safe, secure and private access to their personal health records and also participate in different voting activities. An insightful coverage of Estonia's Blockchain implementation is provided at the following link:

https://www.ctga.ox.ac.uk/sites/default/files/ctga/documents/media/wp7_martinovickellosluganovic.pdf

2.12 Learning from the Aviation Industry

Ever tried entering an airplane, for that matter even gate-crash into an airport without being a ticket-holding passenger?

In many ways, Air travel and Blockchain applications have many things in common. Getting into an airport and into an airplane requires multiple authorizations and checks.

This is like transacting on a Blockchain platform where you need to have accredited identities approved by the network. The passengers going inside have to prove their identities using acknowledged identifiers. The airlines identify the passengers with their PNR (Passenger Name record) to generate the boarding pass that allows one to board the plane. In a similar way, the Blockchain system puts in place multiple identity checks to qualify those who can conduct transactions on the platform that offers a heightened level of security.

Assume you are carrying baggage into the airplane. You have light baggage and heavy baggage. The light baggage can be carried into the plane as cabin baggage while the heavy baggage can be put safely and securely into the luggage compartment. You also need to transport large packets from your location to the destination. It is too expensive to carry such items on the flights. For such stuff, we normally use external transport carriers or couriers once again identifying the consignment with a waybill rather than a proof of carriage of every item individually.

The Blockchain ledger is similarly useful for storing limited payloads (of the first two types mentioned above) wherein some data is a part of the transaction and for larger files to be stored on the Blockchain, a separate but costlier storage medium is used. Anything above a limit must be transacted outside the system or stored in an external Mongo/IPFS database and referenced through its hash onto the system. The privacy of the bag sent into the luggage compartment is secured through a 'baggage tag' with an identifier provided to you and does not require you to prove your identity and the knowledge of the goods, all over. The consignment note sent with the transported/couriered goods is identified by the small tiny piece of associated paper and not by the revelation of the knowledge of the entire goods list inside the packing.

This is like the Zero-Knowledge Proof of a Blockchain that protects the privacy of one's information on a Blockchain. The baggage tag connects the package with the owner passenger, similar to the ZKP identifying the member without having to disclose confidential information thus protecting the privacy.

In cryptography, a zero-knowledge proof or zero-knowledge protocol is a method by which one party (the prover) can prove to another party (the verifier) that they know a value x, without conveying any information apart from the fact that they know the value x. The essence of zero-knowledge proofs is that it is trivial to prove that one possesses knowledge of certain information by simply revealing it; the challenge is to prove such possession without revealing the information itself or any additional information. (Source: Wikipedia)

Assuming you are hopping across different airports, each of the journeys is secured by a time-stamp on the boarding pass identifying the passenger for every leg as he/she enters a new plane.

In the case of an international journey, every entry into and out of the airport is time-stamped and permanently notified on one's passport.

Emigration and Immigration are areas, where Blockchain application is used by many countries. The Emigration and Immigration authorities cross-check the passport of the passenger presented to them with the one recorded on the Blockchain platform managed by the respective Governments for the authenticity of the passenger and the VISA stamp as the case may be. Any tampering of records will be immediately highlighted.

Similarly, in a Blockchain, any asset that moves across different actors is stamped and recorded for every one of its entries and the final consumer can track the entire journey by scanning the QR code that records the movement across various actors in the platform.

Airplane manufacturing majors like Boeing are known to extensively use Blockchain for tracking the provenance, authenticity and usage of their spares across the lifetime to ensure no chances are ever taken in ensuring perfect quality. Boeing is assisted by the technology leader Honeywell to trade its excess spare part inventory in a trusted manner by using GoDirect Trade, a Hyperledger Fabric-based open-sourced Blockchain platform designed to prove the origin of the parts.

'Loyalty points' is another area where Blockchain is used by airplane carriers. Air carriers extensively use networks and try their best to tie up frequent travelers to their own networks. Loyalty points accrued across various journeys in a network act as a glue to make frequent passengers loyal. Singapore Airlines is experimenting with Blockchain for its loyalty program, KrisPay. By leveraging the capabilities of Microsoft Azure's Blockchain as a service, Singapore's national carrier has offered KrisPay, the world's first Blockchain-based airline loyalty digital miles wallet to accumulate their loyalty points into KrisPay miles that can be redeemed any time of their life for attractive rewards in their partner outlets from their mobile phone.

3

PROMISE OF BLOCKCHAIN

Provenance, Authenticity, Trust and Sustained Development

3.1 Book Combines Encryption, Encoding, Hashing, PKI, Timestamps, DSA and Broadcast for the Internet of Value—Privacy, Permission, Passwords

How it all started—Bitcoin, the first implementation of the Blockchain paradigm.

Blockchain technology was demonstrated successfully through its first use case, 'Bitcoin.'

Bitcoin Blockchain is a living example to show that this often-doubted and misunderstood technology is a new paradigm that has come to stay with us for a very long term.

Bitcoin is the first implementation of Blockchain technology consisting of six primary elements:

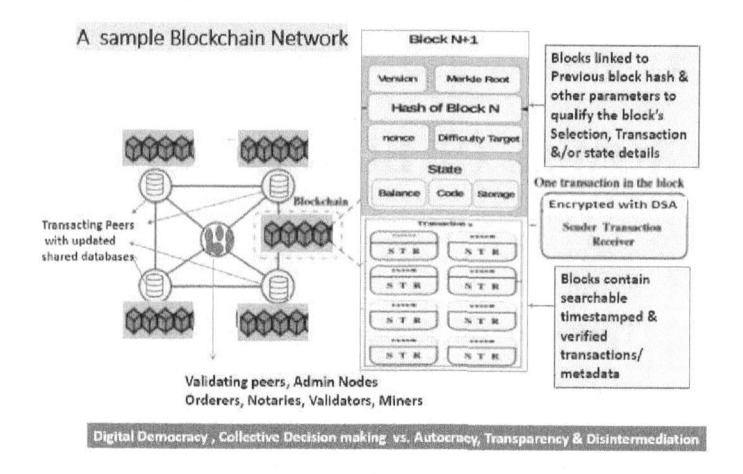

Fig 3.1 A Sample Blockchain Network.

A. An updated Distributed ledger replicated across all the peers undertaking transactions through the platform, consisting of the updated status of Unspent Outputs (UTXO) in chronological order.

B. A network of nodes undertaking to verify and propagate the transactions generated by the participants.

C. A group of miners dispersed across the world to mine the transactions to ensure the authenticity of the same, maintaining the integrity of the Blockchain for all times to come, using an automated execution of the protocol defined by the consensus algorithm called 'Proof-of-Work.' 'Proof-of-Work' represents the amount of work that the miners undertake by utilizing their computing power and electricity spent, to be eligible for block rewards in the form of newly mined coins as per a pre-defined formula.

D. Blockchain wallets used by the participants to initiate transactions and store the value in the form of UTXOs or unspent transaction outputs measured in the number of Bitcoins.

E. The value that is exchanged across the platform, namely the 'Bitcoin' or its fraction, which is treated as a cryptocurrency with all the properties that we associate with the fiat currency in the real world, except the unitized physical representation and regulatory approvals.

F. Exchanges that facilitate buying and selling of cryptocurrencies and derived products known as tokens among themselves using wallets and conversion of the same into fiat currencies in a dynamic manner.

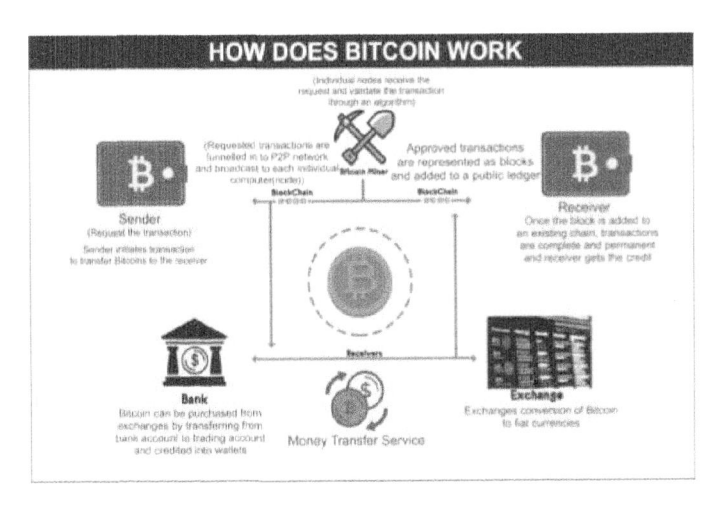

Fig 3.2 How Does Bitcoin Work.

Bitcoin has proved that billions of dollars' worth of value can be exchanged across the world from one person to another unknown person, without the need of a trusted central party, a bank or Government in this case. As on 2nd April 2020, over 18 million Bitcoins with an approximate total value of over 120 billion US Dollar at a unit price of over 6500 US Dollars are in circulation.

The success of Bitcoin led to the launch of several variations of alternate Blockchains for a variety of purposes. The majority of them are cryptocurrencies with different properties in terms of privacy, speed of execution, consensus mechanism for transaction validation, the most prominent variation was proposed in the form of the Ethereum Blockchain platform by Vitalik Buterin and his team at Ethereum foundation.

Ethereum allowed businesses to create decentralized versions of real-life applications that we see in the day-to-day world through the implementation of 'Smart Contracts' which are programs created to replicate the business agreements into applications that can be run on Blockchain databases.

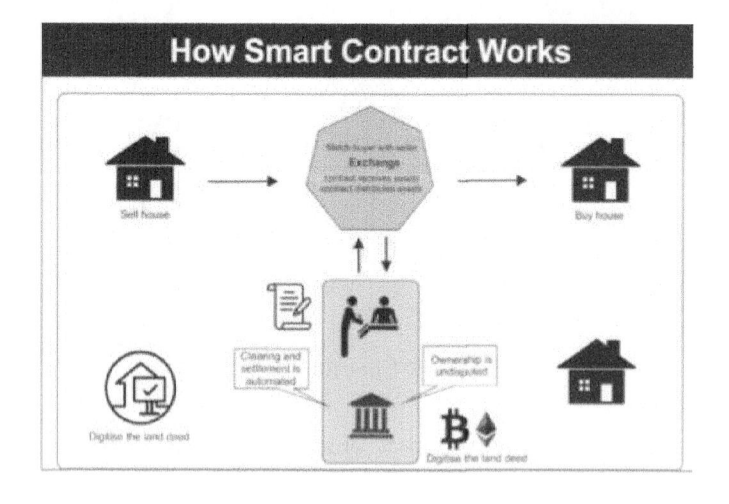

Fig 3.3 How Smart Contract Works.

Enterprise Blockchain platforms like Hyperledger Fabric, Quorum, etc., were developed as variations of the Ethereum platform while enterprise applications like Multichain and R3 Corda took inspiration from the architecture and other elements of Bitcoin Blockchain.

Blockchain converts the traditional internet infrastructure as we know through its TCP/IP protocol from the Internet of Information to the Internet of Value, by acting as a Trusted Third Party to any peer-to-peer interactions. The features of Blockchain that facilitate this are shown in the following figure.

Blockchain Combines Encryption, Encoding, Hashing, PKI, Timestamps, DSA and Broadcast for the Internet of Value by bringing Privacy, Permission, Password management within the reach of an individual peer and frees him/her from the dependence on the Trust Anchors who have now grown unduly large leading to a centralized internet.

74 ♦ *Blockchain for Non IT Professionals*

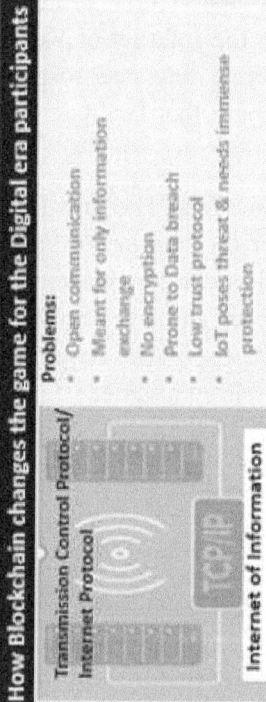

How Blockchain changes the game for the Digital era participants

Transmission Control Protocol/Internet Protocol

Problems:
- Open communication
- Meant for only information exchange
- No encryption
- Prone to Data breach
- Low trust protocol
- IoT poses threat & needs immense protection

Internet of Information

Blockchain Layer over TCP/IP
Encryption, Digital Signatures
Permission & Access rights,
Smart contract capability
Privacy using ZK SNARK,
Homomorphic encryptions for non repudiation in
Peer to Peer Interactions

Solutions:
- Encrypted Point to Point communication
- Secured value exchange at scale
- Ensures Data integrity through hashing
- Pseudonymised / anonymised, distributed ledger eliminates ransomware risks
- Automated trust for disintermediation as Trusted 3rd Party
- Makes IoT devices secure enabling scaled automation & safe M2M (machine to machine interactions)
- High quality data for AI & ML led analytics

Internet for Value Exchange

DISINTERMEDIATING TRUST -- EMPOWERING INDIVIDUAL USERS – FACILITATING SECURE & PRIVATE PEER TO PEER P2P (PERSON TO PERSON), M2M (MACHINE TO PERSON), M2P TRANSACTIONS

Fig 3.4 How Blockchain changes the game for the Digital Era Participants.

Encryption - Encoding - Hashing

Encryption :

Encryption (Symmetric with a common Private key between two persons exchanging information and Asymmetric with different Private Keys is an encoding technique in which message is encoded by using encryption algorithm in such a way that only authorized personnel with the corresponding secret keys can access the message or information.

Encoding :

Encoding transforms data from one form to another so that the same is readable by most of the systems or any other external process. It is like a language translator. Example: ASCII, BASE64, UNICODE

Hashing :

Hash function is a non-reversible technique used to convert data of arbitrary size to data of fixed size number. Popular hashing algorithms like RIPMED, MD5, SHA256. etc., are used to create 'Fingerprint' like record for any data that is stored in a data structure called hash table in a Key-value pair format. Hash produces unique outputs for different inputs and is the best tool to verify Data integrity

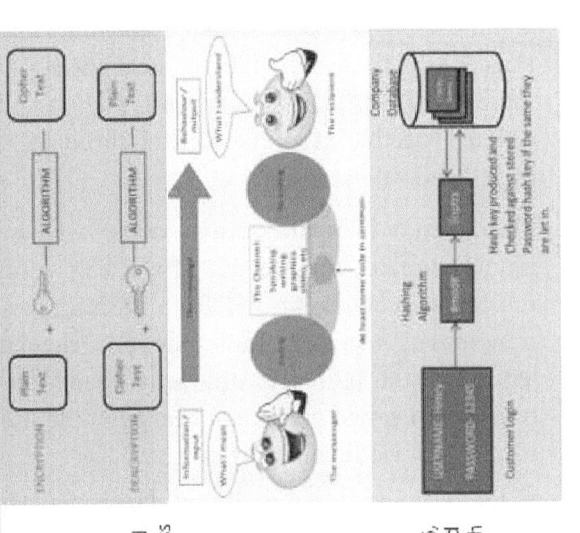

Fig 3.5 Encryption – Encoding – Hashing.

I. **Hash function:** A hash function produces a unique output for a given input, which cannot be replicated. Hash of any information is treated as the unique and indisputable representation of the information. Hashes form the heart of Blockchain as the blocks are represented by the hash of the information and are chained together as a linked list of chronologically mined and validated blocks.

II. **Merkle root (Root of roots):** While a hash is a unique number derived out of the base number, the Merkle root is derived from hashing pairs of transactions together until only one element is left. Since the hash was unique, a change in any transaction would result in a change in the Merkle root, which would be easily caught.

III. **Public-Key Infrastructure:** To facilitate secure electronic transmission of information and undertake ultra-safe transactions, Blockchain employs several cryptographic applications.

PKI or Public-Key Infrastructure is a set of technological procedures used to create, manage, distribute, use, store, and revoke digital certificates. PKI is used to authenticate participating parties using public keys and corresponding private keys connected to each other through complex algorithmic relations, requiring rigorous proofs to confirm identities for facilitating information exchange. PKI uses X.509 certificates to identify the owners of public keys.

   a. **Private key and Public-Key:** The Private Key and Public-Key are used to encrypt information using mathematical algorithms, rendering decryption virtually impossible without these keys. Computationally, it is similar to the factoring of prime numbers, which is a simple, mathematical procedure. However, decomposing the result is difficult without prior knowledge of its factors.

b. **RSA:** PKI systems normally use RSA algorithms for linking public keys and private keys. RSA (Revest–Shamir–Adleman) is one of the first public-key cryptosystems and is widely used for secure data transmission. In such a cryptosystem, the encryption key is public and it is different from the decryption key which is kept secret (private).

c. **ECDSA:** Blockchain systems use Elliptical curve cryptography to issue secure Public-key-Private key pairs. The messages are encrypted by a digital signature algorithm namely, ECDSA that ensures that only authorized owners of targeted messages are able to securely decrypt the messages.

IV. **Digital Signatures:** Digital signatures are a unique aspect of Blockchain transactions and provide a layer of security to carry out and validate genuine transactions. A digital signature is a mathematical scheme to present the authenticity of digital messages or documents. A valid digital signature gives the recipient reason to believe that the message was created by a known sender (authentication), and the sender cannot deny having sent the message (non-repudiation), or that the message was not altered in transit.

V. Consensus Mechanisms (POW, POS, DPOS, PBFT, etc.): The mechanism by which members come to an agreement about the authenticity of a transaction is referred to as the 'Consensus Mechanism.' Consensus formation ensures the involvement of multiple validators in a systematic and predetermined manner, ensuring decentralization and objectivity of decision-making. It ensures implementation of the key features of the Blockchain platform like increased trust, immutability of the transactions, and maintenance of the integrity of the platform.

The consensus mechanism is the soul of the Blockchain platform and has to help members in reaching the right decision all the time. The sanctity of the Blockchain application depends on the strength and reliability of the consensus mechanism. The consensus mechanism followed by Bitcoin and the earlier version of the public Ethereum client is known as 'Proof-of-Work (POW)' where miners or validators compete with each other and burn valuable resources like computing power and enormous amounts of electricity to guess the right Nonce (number used only once) and create a targeted hash to win the race to create a block.

Proof-of-Work—followed by Bitcoin Blockchain and some versions of Ethereum Blockchain—consumes a huge amount of resources to arrive at a deterministic consensus. The Ethereum platform will soon shift to a 'Proof of Stake'-based consensus, which involves negligible energy consumption.

Some new-generation public platforms use variations of 'POW' – and 'POS'-based consensus algorithms like PoET (Proof of Elapsed Time) and DPOS (Delegated Proof of Stake) to minimize resource utilization and wastage.

Enterprise Blockchains use energy-efficient algorithms like 'Proof of Authority' (POA), Practical Byzantine Fault-Tolerant' (PBFT), 'Node to Node' (N2N) and their variations to arrive at a deterministic consensus.

Blockchain's Magical Components:

MAGIC CALLED BLOCKCHAIN

Fair & Transparent Cooperative style Governance with a Win for all approach

Incentives to participate in decisions through high ROI or network currency

Cryptographic security Through Hashing, encoding, Digital signatures & Privacy protocols

State of art Messaging, Streaming, Caching & Storage systems for synchronisation & Fault tolerance & API management

BLOCKCHAIN'S MAGICAL COMPONENTS A COMBINATION OF MANY SIMPLE CONCEPTS FOR A BRILLIANT EFFECT

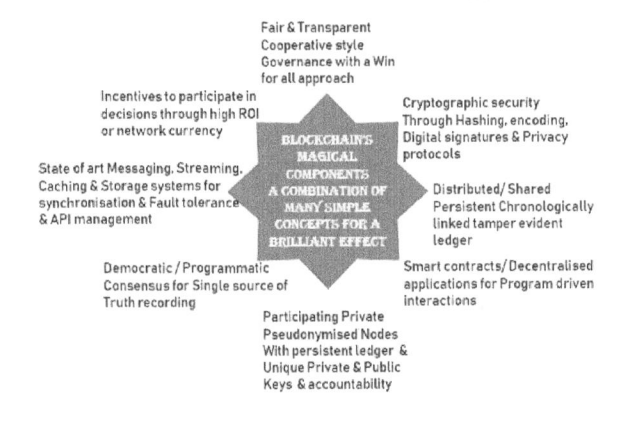

Distributed/Shared Persistent Chronologically linked tamper evident ledger

Democratic/Programmatic Consensus for Single source of Truth recording

Smart contracts/Decentralised applications for Program driven interactions

Participating Private Pseudonymised Nodes With persistent ledger & Unique Private & Public Keys & accountability

Fig 3.6 Magic Called Blockchain.

As seen in the above section the discovery of the Blockchain paradigm has been achieved by an ingenious combination of the various simple tools and techniques that have been in vogue for decades.

3.2 Say No to Fakes

The fake goods menace across the Pharma, Auto components, Precious goods and high-quality exported goods is fueling the need for 'Authenticity confirming' solutions that enable tracking the source of origin of goods, a facility very much offered by the Enterprise Blockchain applications. This had further found applications in areas like marine products, farm and other food products that can be tracked through the supply chain across multiple enterprises, by Blockchain platforms that are making these look simple by abstracting several components of these solutions through sophisticated smart contracts and ingeniously implemented consensus protocols.

Blockchain is now seen as the savior to stop the death of over a hundred and twenty thousand citizens across Africa alone to spurious drugs and save over 77 Billion US Dollars annually to the US health care industry. Global giants across the Pharma domain and even food giants like Walmart are exploring Blockchain technology across their organizations and ecosystems.

The mistrust governing academic certificates, land records, licenses and health records behind insurance claims has not been conclusively addressed until the advent of the Blockchain paradigm.

Blockchain-based KYC, citizen and customer identity records and certificates from birth to academic, extracurricular, medical, to property ownership to marriage till death are now deemed to be immutably and permanently recorded on Blockchain eliminating the need to carry sheets of untrusted paper-based records.

Blockchain solutions to eliminate the Fake products and documents menace

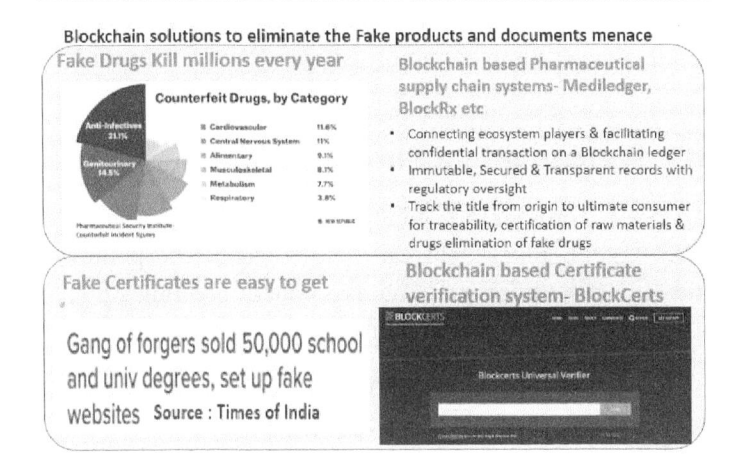

Fake Drugs Kill millions every year

Counterfeit Drugs, by Category

Blockchain based Pharmaceutical supply chain systems- Mediledger, BlockRx etc

- Connecting ecosystem players & facilitating confidential transaction on a Blockchain ledger
- Immutable, Secured & Transparent records with regulatory oversight
- Track the title from origin to ultimate consumer for traceability, certification of raw materials & drugs elimination of fake drugs

Fake Certificates are easy to get

Gang of forgers sold 50,000 school and univ degrees, set up fake websites Source : Times of India

Blockchain based Certificate verification system- BlockCerts

Fig 3.7 Blockchain Solutions to Eliminate the Fake Products and Documents Menace.

Countries like Estonia, Switzerland, Singapore are showing the way and economically significant and advanced nations like Dubai and other middle east countries are embracing the 'Blockchain paradigm' with all hands and are planning to go paperless by 2020.

With Permanence (Immutability of records), Authenticity (Provenance and proof of ownership) and Trust (Trust guaranteed by peer-to-peer autonomous organizations created through Smart Contracts), adopting Blockchains seem to be the way to go boosting your 'PAT' and gain the much needed competitive advantage in the 'Automated' world of the coming era of 'Innoruption' or innovation-led disruption!

Blockchain is thus seen as a great platform that can hasten the world's quest to meet the Sustainable Development Goals for 2030, mandated by the United

Nations General Assembly in 2015. (Source: https://sustainabledevelopment.un.org/sdgs)

3.3 Welcome to a Pure World

We often come across adulterated food and a polluted environment. Blockchain can help to track the pollution and effluent guzzlers and help the state in creating a policy of incentivizing or penal actions against errant actors.

The following diagram gives a schema for implementing such a Blockchain-based decentralized application. Implementation of CBDC (Central Bank Digital Currency) over a DLT platform can support such actions that can lead to a purer environment and assist in achieving Sustainable Development Goals.

Central bank digital currency (CBDC) is the digital form of fiat_money (a currency established as money by Government regulation, monetary authority or law). (Wikipedia)

CBDC, when administered by the Governments over a Permissioned Blockchain, facilitates the speedy and efficient exchange of value across transacting parties across the globe and also provides the added benefit of trust, transparency, non-repudiation and security. This also can pave the way for an efficient cross-border inter-bank remittance between any connected entities whether human beings or 'things.'

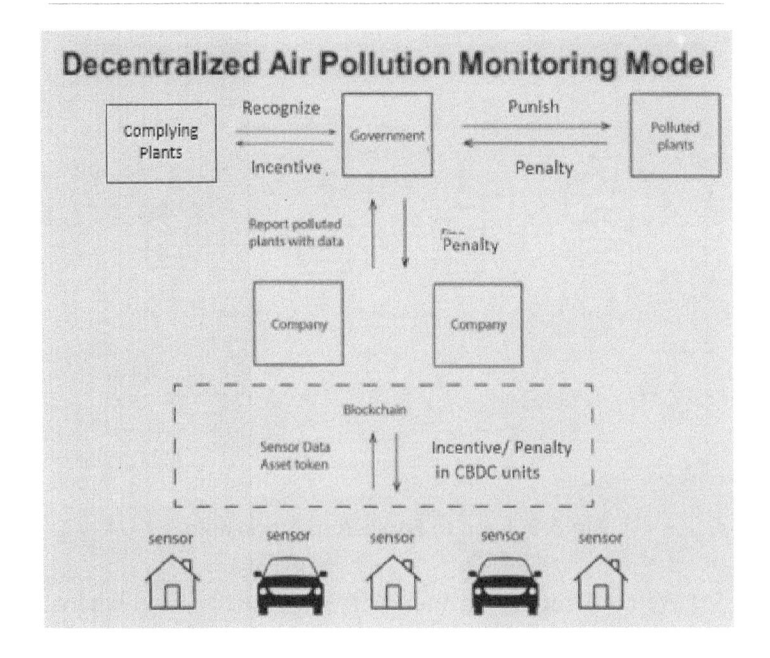

Fig 3.8 Decentralized Air Pollution Monitoring Model.

Blockchain helps to track the source of contaminated food which in turn keeps a check on those responsible for sourcing and transporting food items. In agriculture, the crop production can be tracked from farm to fork, ensuring along the way using the IOT technology to monitor storage conditions like temperature, etc. to ensure that it is not spoiled on the way.

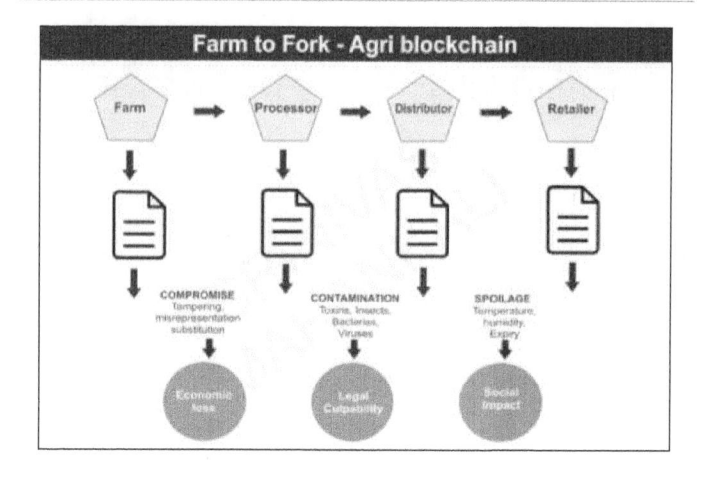

Fig 3.9 Farm to Fork—Agri Blockchain.

We are living in an increasingly polluted world where the natural resources are depleting by the day and the natural energy resources while depleting are also resulting in several environmental issues. Trees are being felled and forests are vanishing, the quality of water, air and the entire atmosphere is slowly turning for the worse even as the population has grown five times in the past 100 years!

There have been several initiatives that are facilitating renewable energy resource generation and trading leading to substantial accrual of Carbon credits. Blockchain supports renewable energy generation and trading of the same between Prosumer and consumers on a one-to-one basis. Further, it will enable us to track the exact percentage of renewable energy being used by the consumers and compare them with the benchmarks whether regulatory or otherwise. The following figure gives a schema for a Blockchain application for renewable energy trading.

Energy trading is another opportunity that is increasingly viewed for Blockchain adaption.

The producers of energy will be able to confidently trade their excess produce with the consumers in need of the same. Smart contracts can provide for listing, discovery, trading, settlement of all transactions pertaining to energy trading among the generators and users.

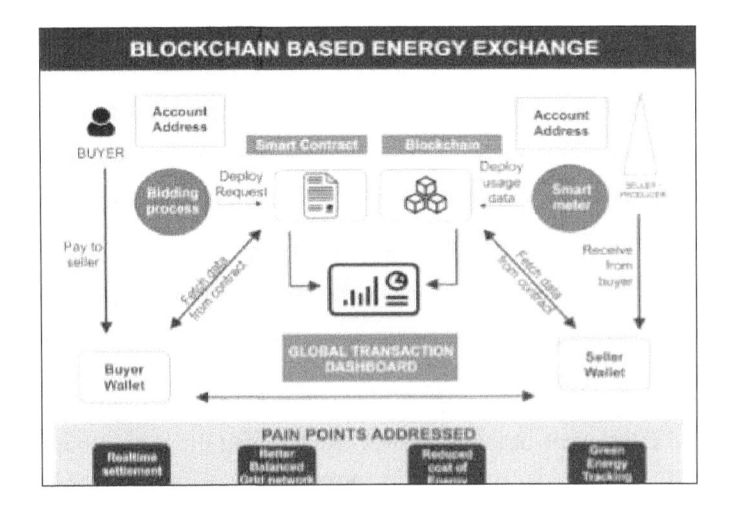

Fig 3.10 Blockchain-Based Energy Exchange.

Another important initiative to watch out for is the efforts at climate preservation being done by Blockchain Start-ups across the world.

The Most Influential People of African Descent (MIPAD), a group working in Africa is trying to get the rich non-resident Africans to help afforestation activities in the continent and help them monitor the progress of the trees over a Blockchain network. MIPAD and Decagon Institute are leveraging Artificial intelligence and machine learning to geo-tag and monitor the trees planted and tracked through a Distributed ledger.

Unique tagging and identification on Google maps give the assurance to the investors of the trees to keep track and monitor their progress with utmost trust. This will encourage the investors to subscribe to more and more trees and reach the objective of planting over 200 million trees by 2024.

More such projects will help in afforestation in the world and lead to a pure environment by enabling us to reach the goals of Sustainable Development.

3.4 Say no to Middlemen— Disintermediation

Bitcoin Blockchain empowered its members to create units of value called Bitcoin cryptocurrency and allowed them to transfer between themselves without any intermediaries while the Blockchain acted like a Trusted Third Party. Just like an internet-based telephone call that can directly connect two individuals unlike the normal telephone networks that need to do multiple hops, the Blockchain enables the members to trade value instantaneously over the net, unlike the normal central bank-backed physical currency system.

Thus Blockchain offers an opportunity to eliminate the role of often expensive and time-consuming middleperson-related processes.

World Food Program demonstrated the effectiveness of Blockchain in eliminating several low values adding intermediaries while transferring aid to refugees.

World Food Program's Aid disbursements to Syrian Refugees:

The World Food Program has created a private Blockchain fork of Ethereum with the help of an engineering firm parity and is transferring the aid to the Syrian refugees directly through Blockchain.

Before:

World Food Program used to provide vouchers on account of aid provided to the refugees, which they used to encash in the retail outlets and supermarkets against their purchases. This amounted to huge leakages on account of wrong voucher submissions, bank charge and time delays.

Now:

With the help of the Blockchain, the refugees are provided accounts on the Blockchain, identified by their scanned images of their Iris by the World Food Program. Now, upon purchasing any items at the supermarkets, the refugees are identified by iris scanners by the supermarket staff and the due amounts debited to the World Food Program are credited to the supermarkets on account of the respective refugee's account.

This has saved the WFP over 98% in banks and other financial charges and now, they have a plan to spread it to refugees across all the regions over a variety of services.

3.5 No More Corruption

On 29th January 2018, one of the leading public sector banks of India discovered that a couple of its employees colluded with some large clients to defraud the bank of over INR 14356 Crores (US Dollar 2 Billion).

(https://en.wikipedia.org/wiki/Punjab_National_Bank_Scam). This was the outcome of the fraudulent behavior of the employees who undertook forgery and also undermined the banking system to allow these transactions to take place. This crime would not have taken place if there was a foolproof system of accountability and digital signatures enforced by a system, coupled with the intractability of tamper-evident transactions. This is what is made possible by Blockchain.

We have seen that in Permissioned Blockchains, implementation and adherence to excellent KYC/AML regulations and management of authorized member identities through accredited MSP (Membership Service Providers) ensures that any mistakes done in the system could be identified easily and attributed to the member's real identity easily.

Once recorded with the time-stamp, since it is impossible to delete the record, the propensity to undertake any illegal and irresponsible transactions, the system will be able to trace the events to the precise event recorded and the identity responsible for the same.

This ensures that virtually no one dares to take a risk and commit any misdeed or wrongful and malicious activities on the system. This is like a CCTV camera installed in a premise that not only continuously records and tracks the event, but also ensures that the data can never be altered or deleted.

In real life we have seen several cases, corruption is the result of irresponsible and criminal minded professionals in a centralized system, forging signatures or undertaking surreptitious activities and pushing through transactions that are not authorized and later tampering the records to hide their misdeeds.

Implementation of Blockchain in land records management eliminates several disputes related to illegal land transfers and also a number of murderous disputes in land titling and ownership claims.

Several countries like Dubai, UK, Sweden have already implemented land records management on Blockchain.

Fig 3.11 Land Title Deed stored on a Blockchain by Dubai Government one of the best exponents of disruptive technologies.

The use of Blockchain ensures that no unauthorized activity is ever undertaken unless approved by the application or the Smart Contract and also the necessary signatures are appended to the transaction in the form of digital signature algorithms and signature cryptographically attested with the private key. This eliminates the possibility of corruption in any transaction.

3.6 Break the back of Cybercriminals

In late April 2007, a series of cyber-attacks were conducted on the Government and public sites of Estonia, a small European country that was formed out of erstwhile USSR. They targeted websites of Estonians, including Estonian parliament, banks, ministries, newspapers and broadcasters, amid the country's disagreement with Russia about the relocation of the Bronze Soldier of Tallinn, an elaborate Soviet-era grave marker, as well as war graves in Tallinn.

Estonia today is one of the most digitally advanced nations in the world and has implemented an impeccable cyber defense strategy to secure all the records of the Government and those of its citizens and the business community. Estonia implemented a Blockchain platform that provides complete data integrity for all its transactions across its entire infrastructure. This has led to a complete reduction in any such wrongful cyber incidents on its soil.

In June 2017, A.P. Moller-Maersk, the world's largest Container shipping company fell victim to a major cyber-attack caused by the Not Petya malware, which also affected many organizations globally. As a result, Maersk's operations in transport and logistics businesses were disrupted, leading to unwarranted impact. This led to a loss of over 300 Million US$ in business losses, restoration losses and other collateral damages.

The response to the cyber-attack was a multipronged proactive approach to implement an impeccable cyber defense strategy to protect the organizations against such attacks in the future.

This has led to the formation of TradeLens, a Blockchain consortium as a joint venture with IBM, the global leader in Blockchain solutions and infrastructure to make global trade more efficient, transparent and secure. Today, more than 60% of the global trade of containers is tracked through the TradeLens platform.

By its ability to have multiple levels of checks for access, authentication and authorization, decentralized decision-making to approve transactions to modify ledgers, Blockchain significantly enhances the cyber resilience of the systems and makes it impenetrable to cybercriminals. Thus, the Return-on-Investments for cybercriminals is substantially reduced or becomes non-remunerative.

However, any defects in the Smart Contract applications or third-party related infrastructure, (like wallets, exchanges) especially in the Permissionless Blockchains like Bitcoin and Ethereum, can create irreversible loss and needs to be guarded against.

3.7 Go for the Goals (SDG)

The Sustainable Development Goals are a collection of 17 global goals designed to be a "blueprint to achieve a better and more sustainable future for all". The SDGs, set in 2015 by the United Nations General Assembly and intended to be achieved by the year 2030, is part of UN Resolution 70/1, the 2030 Agenda. (Wikipedia)

Sustainable Development Goals

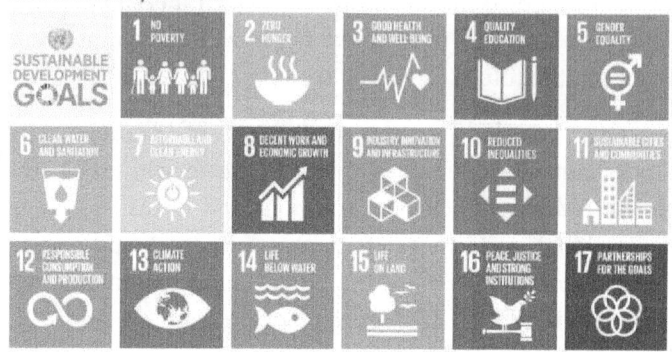

Fig 3.12 Sustainable Development Goals: Source: https://sustainabledevelopment.un.org/sdgs

Blockchain has helped in a multipronged approach to attain the Sustainable Development Goals by all nations. The utility of Blockchain for the same is given as follows.

1. Eliminate Poverty: Targeted Govt. benefits to poor persons with no leakages.

2. Eliminate Hunger: Support Humanitarian activities targeted at food distribution in a coordinated manner. Crowdsource and track information on people deprived of daily minimum needs. World Food Program, an example.

3. Good health and well-being: Track medical records, eliminate fake drugs, support clinical trials and Pharma research and deliver and monitor high-quality subsidized cheap drugs. Track immunization

health records of children through their early life. Insurance for all, especially pregnant women, elderly, poor and vulnerable tracked through Blockchain.

4. Quality education: Track academic credentials on Blockchain and support brilliant and downtrodden through scholarships and the right opportunities for global exposure of talent of them and to them.

5. Gender Equality: Incentivize and reward organizations and regions showing better performance on gender parity in areas like board rooms, staff ratio and Woman safety. Offer a channel for new employment opportunities for women with career breaks and with handicaps. Track safety measures and actions against atrocities for women in a coordinated manner.

6. Clean water and sanitation: Tracking effluents of industry, water pollution levels of major river bodies, the health of lakes, utilization of budgets targeted for Water conservation, Rainwater harvesting track records and efforts, etc.

7. Clean renewable energy: Enable peer-to-peer renewable energy trading, Reward renewable energy consumption, Track carbon certificates, facilitate measurement of usage and generation.

8. Sustainable employment: Verified expertise credentials and facilitate the gig economy for trusted peer-to-peer project marketplace

9. Innovation, industrialization, and infrastructure: Protect patents and help share and monetize

intellectual capital. 3D manufacturing for productive industries and fast deployments, encourage recycling and reuse of industrial waste and residue.

10. Reduce country-level inequalities: Cross-country global cooperation, resource trading with reduced costs and complexities.

11. Safe Smart Cities: Secure IOT infrastructure with Blockchain for scalable automation.

12. Responsible Production and consumption: Tracking supply chains for ethical sourcing and providing live accurate data for forecasting.

13. Climate action: Track and reward environment conservation actions and progressive improvements across regions for reducing pollution.

14. Life underwater: Track the quality of seawater for harmful effluents and take steps to address deteriorations.

15. Life on land: Track forest fires on a live basis across the world, take steps to track and improve afforestation, check desertification, aid in disaster management activities through coordinated actions.

16. Peace, Justice and Strong Institutions ID2020 and Digital Identities. Blockchains enable trust which would, in turn, help mitigate corruption.

17. Partnerships—global partnerships with win-win associations with collaboration, coordination, communication, cooperation facilitated by Blockchain.

3.8 All the Possibilities to Track

Blockchain's key applications are well be summarized in the following figure:

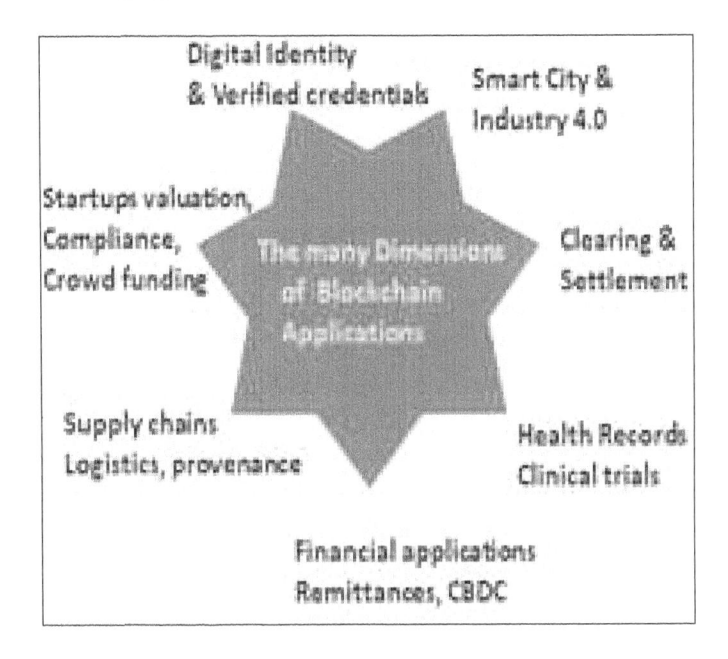

Fig: **3.13** Key applications of Blockchain.

Blockchain's value proposition across industries and use cases

Government

PROBLEM: Governments offer numerous certificates of identification and authenticity to their citizens. They are the biggest spenders of public money, collector of taxes and distribute subsidies. Governments also undertake large projects on an ongoing basis inside the country and outside the country through the External Affairs Ministry, Government has to implement Smart City projects and provide cybersecurity to critical installations. All these areas are fraught with complexity and potential fraud leading to a lot of leakage and loss of money on a huge scale.

SOLUTION OFFERED BY BLOCKCHAIN

By offering foolproof methods for issuing unique digital identities, ensuring the provenance of goods and supplies, providing certificates registered on a Blockchain and ensuring accountability and transparency in project management, procurement, vendor management and supply chains through non-refutable digital signatures and immutably stored data that cannot be manipulated and modified, Governments stand to save a huge portion of their expenses while delighting the citizens. After citizens demand transparency, efficiency, ease of interactions and lower costs that Blockchain's dis-intermediated trust can offer as a de-facto outcome!

Project Management

PROBLEMS: Project Management involves the delivery of expected and planned outcomes through the utilization of defined and budgeted resources comprising of money, manpower, materials and time.

This involves interactions between multiple parties both inside and extraneous to organizations and the results are dependent on multiple parties working strictly in consonance to their contracts with the implementation. Most often, the lack of synchronization between parties concerned and participants falling short of their deliverables lead to cost and time overruns and humongous losses throwing all the plans awry.

SOLUTION OFFERED BY BLOCKCHAIN

Recording the Contracts and monitoring the project status and adherence to the deliverables in the same manner by all the parties concerned as per milestones is best done over a Blockchain platform to ensure compliance.

Cryptographic references to project status are stored on the Blockchain and the status report with respect to the deliverables are shared periodically and on critical matters shared over the Distributed ledgers in real-time. The tamper-evident nature of the records and the 'Triple entry-accounting' feature of the Blockchain acting as a Trusted Third Party will ensure that the accountability of all concerned parties is monitored in a foolproof manner for timely action and also to dispense rewards/penalties required to put the projections execution ahead of schedule on all dimensions.

Transparent procurement process-automated bid management with details of successful vendors recorded on a Blockchain and monitoring the progress of their deliveries can also trigger delivery versus payments in a trusted manner with the highest accountability of the involved officials, thus eliminating chances of errors and misappropriation as well.

Digital Identity

PROBLEMS: Multiple records, Duplication of efforts and processes, Siloed systems and potential for identity fraud and that of stolen credential copies.

SOLUTION OFFERED BY BLOCKCHAIN

Issue and verify once on Blockchain, link multiple identities to a unique Blockchain identity-operated through a single user interface or a digital wallet, eliminate the need for multiple verifications across establishments thus saving a lot of time, effort and documentations which maximizes the trustworthiness of the identity information.

Voting

PROBLEM: Tedious manual paper and printing intensive processes requiring humongous funds and fake/unaccounted identities pose enormous challenges for countries and enterprises undertaking elections for governing bodies and on-board resolutions.

SOLUTION OFFERED BY BLOCKCHAIN

By uniquely identifying voters in a foolproof manner and recording their votes through their digital signatures through a verifiable and non-refutable system, Blockchain eliminates fake votes, wrong votes and extensive paperwork eliminating wasteful processes to reduce costs enormously.

Registries and Certificates

PROBLEM: Fake certificates and high cost and time required for issuance and verification plague documentation of events from birth to will execution for asset acquisition and credential accumulation.

SOLUTION OFFERED BY BLOCKCHAIN

Educational Municipal, Police and other credential certificates can be issued and shared securely eliminating fakes and offering benefits for instant audit and reconciliation while establishing clear title.

Benefits and Subsidy Distribution

PROBLEM: Fake claims, excessive middle layers leading to leakages and adding non-value costs drain valuable resources of Government and trusts.

SOLUTION OFFERED BY BLOCKCHAIN

Clear identification of beneficiaries, allotment and monitoring of benefit utilization for every unit issued with minimal intermediary intervention in near real-time allows for high productivity of welfare spends.

Supply Chain

PROBLEM:

Procurement: Subjectivity and opaque procurement processes create leakages and mistrust.

Financial Documentation: Letter of Credit, Suppliers credit and other financial transactions offer a lot of scope for manipulation and mistrust.

Provenance: Fake goods and wrong claims for premiumness hamper a variety of goods ranging from Pharma, food, imported, exported and specialized products

Retail: Warranty claims, Loyalty rewards cross multiple vendors are difficult to track and often lead to disputes

Transport conditions: Un-monitored cold storage transported goods like pharmaceuticals, food, milk and dairy products lead to the consumption of spurious/expired products.

SOLUTION OFFERED BY BLOCKCHAIN

Transparent and Trusted processes offered by immutable, shared ledger of records between verified identities.

Digital signatures for non-repudiation and shared ledger for near-real-time communication drastically reduces costs and scope for frauds.

Smart contracts triggered to capture the events like a change of ownership and transfer of assets immutably on a shared ledger, help identify the origin of the products along with certifications of the originality of standard adherence, especially valuable in Automotive spares.

Blockchain facilitates seamless tracking of warranty claims and allotted rewards until redemption for increased effectiveness and benefit of consumers.

By recording the temperature of cold-stored items across the supply chain and tracking them on a Blockchain ledger, the consignment details of spoiled items can be quickly traced. This will minimize the propensity of willful manipulation.

Health Care

PROBLEM: Fake drugs, Compliance in Clinical record management, health record tracking and settlement of insurance claims are often causes for fraud and manipulation.

SOLUTION OFFERED BY BLOCKCHAIN

Blockchain can offer multiple benefits for solving the various challenges of health care domains like seamless management of EHRs with utmost privacy and security features, transparent compliance tracking in case of clinical records and insurance settlement and Origin-to-chemist tracking of Pharma goods, etc.

Smart City

PROBLEM: Unauthorized access by cybercriminals to leverage net connectivity of the IOT devices for DDOS attacks and illegal actions like crypto-jacking, data leaks, etc. The command and control of autonomous vehicles and drones need to be secured against cybercriminals.

SOLUTION OFFERED BY BLOCKCHAIN

Blockchain offers a protective shield for IOT Gateways, autonomous vehicles, drones and robots and prevents unauthorized access by criminals and manipulators. This enables secured automation. Blockchain facilitated accurate assessment of renewable energy claims and peer-to-peer energy trading among Prosumers.

Cybersecurity

PROBLEMS: Single points of failure of centralized management offer valuable targets for cybercriminals. Increasingly digitization and billions of internet connections managed by centralized systems run the risk of derailment and ransom attacks. WannaCry, one such virus infected 230,000 computers in over 150 countries, using 20 different languages took $300 US Dollars per computer to decrypt and release the data.

SOLUTION OFFERED BY BLOCKCHAIN

By sharing distributing data across multiple ledgers, authenticating identities, encrypting transaction information, Blockchain offers a de-risking mechanism for data-intensive applications and blunts designs of Ransomware criminals who fraudulently sneak into corporate systems, encrypt the data and demand ransom to decrypt the same.

The utility of Blockchain in eliminating fakes through trusted document management and ensuring source to destination ownership tracking can be succinctly summarized in the following lifecycle activities that could be authentically stored on a Blockchain:

- **Cradle to Grave/Womb to Tomb** – All certificates in one's life from birth certificates, vaccination records, Health/Property and Academic, Nonacademic and Identity records, Will recording and execution, etc., need impeccable tracking that Blockchain provides.

- **Vivad to Viswas** – Any agreements and compliance issues can be easily reconciled.

- **Farm to Fork/Catch to Consumption** – Safe and compassionate handling of animals and amphibians meant for consumption can be tracked through the supply chain.

- **Procure to Pay** – Complete transparency in the Procurement process by recording activities in every stage. Procurement is the biggest source of subjective behavior that can be made transparent.

- **Pay to Cash** – Manpower and work outsourcing organizations can minimize Pay-Bill cycle leakages by instant settlements and eliminating the need for reconciliation.

- **Admission to Retirement** – Academic and nonacademic certificates and transcripts can be stored and shared privately without any fear of fake certificates and time loss.

- **Segregation of Duties:** In issues of Project management or execution of shared responsibilities in organizations, IT projects and new product development, there is a need for responsible and automated tracking of discharge of one's duties. Digital signatures and non-repudiation help in achieving instant confirmations and recognition of good and productive behavior.

- **Startup valuation and compliance tracking:** Most of the small companies suffer from the inability to capture value contributions and tracking from the promoters and investors. Blockchain enables perfect, real-time valuation, promoter shares' tracking and support in compliance management for the Startup founders from the idea stage itself.

- **Sanction to Settlement:** Many activities in Government and enterprise domains need approvals and endorsement. Blockchain can track the documentation and attestations from approval to settlement in an impeccable manner. House designs, Police approvals for public meetings, large project budgets are some of the many such activities that can benefit from the Blockchain approach.

The following solution depicts a typical document management solution by leveraging Blockchain technology to eliminate fake certificates and facilitate trusted sharing of information guaranteed by Blockchain while protecting from malware attacks and any form of unauthorized tampering.

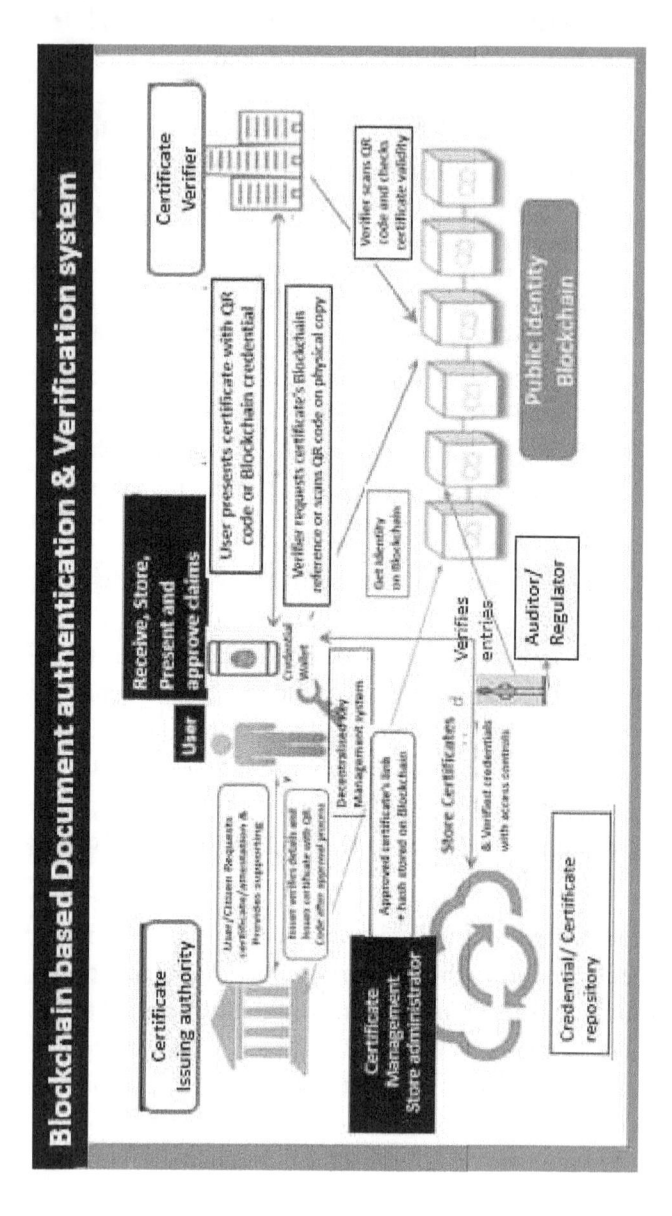

Fig: 3.14 Blockchain-based Instant Document management authenticity verification system.

Loyalty, Games and Sweepstakes and many more applications that depend on Trust are lifelong relationships between hitherto unknown parties cutting across domains, will find Blockchain an interesting platform to adopt and provide value to the peers on either side.

Blockchain can also help in a variety of Smart City applications to save lives and improve quality of life. The following case study showcases the use of Distributed Ledger Technology to seamlessly connect various actors in a smart city ecosystem to improve emergency healthcare response.

1 Collaborative Smart City Emergency Response for Smart cities:

Smart cities in India have implemented various 'smart' elements across several dimensions to automate various aspects of the lifecycle of a citizen's interactions with the Government. To facilitate smooth coordination between the citizens and the smart elements present in the city, ICCC (Integrated Command and Control Center) has been set up by all the smart cities.

However, the communication among all the smart elements is still lacking coordination especially with respect to a timely and coordinated data sharing.

Faced with one of the highest numbers of traffic deaths across all the megacities of India at 157 per hundred thousand of population, Bhopal has sought to leverage Distributed Ledger Technologies to integrate various elements of its Emergency Response actors and their activities.

CHALLENGES IN EMERGENCY RESPONSE MANAGEMENT

Stakeholders involved in Emergency Response Management

The current system lacks synergy within departments due to the following scenarios:

- Emergency services like the 108 ambulance service (operated under the National Health Mission) and departments like the police department exist and operate in silos.
- There are no active communication links between the Ambulance service and the ITMS (Intelligent Traffic Management System) responsible for performing smart traffic management.
- Without prior notice, hospitals are unable to prepare for emergency cases being brought to it by the ambulance

Fig 3.15 Challenges In Emergency Response Management.

By introducing the concept of distributed data ownership, where each stakeholder owns only their data, DEF removes a Single Point of Failure and helps introduce trust among all stakeholders. Stakeholders are able to transparently share information with an immutable audit trail of each transfer The ICCC is able to streamline the city's Emergency Response service with other departments such as the traffic management system, hospitals, surveillance systems and the police.

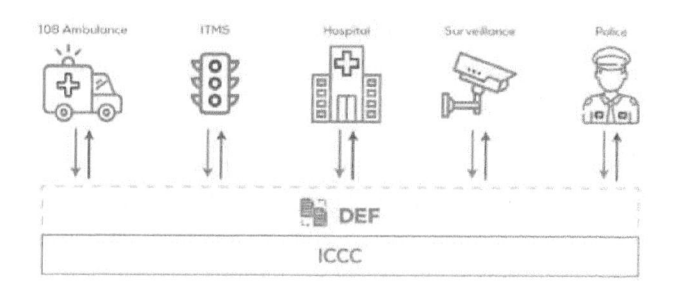

Fig 3.16 Data exchange framework of ICCC to connect all the players in the Emergency Response team (Source: Somish Solutions Ltd.)

By implementing a shared ledger by leveraging Distributed Ledger Technology, the Smart City of Bhopal's ICCC was able to create a rapid response to any emergency by the ambulance service to any accident case that is being reported by the citizens. The process flow is described below:

- The citizen reports an incident via the 108 Helpline.
- As the ambulance is dispatched the case details are shared with the relevant hospital, ensuring the staff has enough time to prepare for the emergency case.
- The ICCC is informed of the incident location and designated hospital, which activates the ITMS to create a traffic-free route leveraging the surveillance, public announcement and traffic management systems.

This establishes coordination among stakeholders, increased inter-department synergy and significantly faster transit time by triggering a green corridor for the ambulance transit.

The Smart City of Bhopal, in association with the Institute of Development Studies and National Institute of Urban Studies, successfully concluded the pilot in collaboration with Somish Solutions Ltd and is planning to expand the pilot for wider implementation.

Case study: Courtesy, Somish Solutions Ltd, New Delhi

Digital Representation of Assets and Rights on a Blockchain vide Tokenization:

As we have seen earlier, the trust in the Blockchain platform which by itself is expected to act like a Disintermediating Trust machine must be above board with a due demonstration of credibility and high credentials. For this, the consortium leading the Blockchain platform's consensus mechanism, acting as the backbone for the entire solution should comprise of many leading stalwarts in the industry who could otherwise be competitors but are acting like collaborators in the Blockchain regime.

The concept of Tokenization is a powerful concept that enables real-life assets and rights to be represented as digital equivalent value units on a Blockchain. Tokenization will enable members of different peer entities (that could be individuals or organizations) to represent their products and service in a common digital unit that could be traded.

Ethereum pioneered the concept of decentralized applications that are powered by the respective Ethereum (native cryptocurrency of Ethereum Public Blockchain) compatible tokens which could be freely traded on the network. This will enable the launch of decentralized versions of all the real-life applications as we know like Amazon, Facebook powered by a Blockchain-based token. LIBRA coin, powered by a Blockchain platform spearheaded by Facebook is a precursor of things to come with respect to migration of today's centralized systems on to a Blockchain-based infrastructure.

Blockchain platform-based applications like LIBRA (promoted by a group with Facebook as the leading member), Hash graph are combining ranks of leading players in the global business ecosystem and Fortune 100 members to form strong governing boards that could act like the 'Trusted Third Party' in a foolproof manner.

LIBRA is a Permissioned Blockchain digital currency proposed by the American social media company Facebook,

Inc. The project, currency and transactions are to be managed and cryptographically entrusted to the LIBRA Association, a membership of companies from payment, technology, telecommunication, online marketplace and venture capital, and nonprofits. (Wikipedia)

Understanding LIBRA coin, JPM Coin and Bitcoin with analogies.

- In our day-to-day life, we use Market place portals like Amazon or malls like Forum mall which have food courts inside that operate like food market place.

- These market places offer tokens in exchange for our money like Amazon Pay Balance Tokens or a food token loaded debit card. We can use these tokens and purchase goods/food items in the respective market place and once we are done with the place, we can exchange it back for the balance money. However, we need to note that all these coins are operated by centralized organizations and not in any way operated by a Blockchain network like Bitcoin. These tokens are only useful within the respective market place ecosystems and cannot be used anywhere else.

- Assuming you want these marketplace specific tokens to be used across several such merchant establishments, there should be an API-based integration and a common Identity across these platforms like PayBack points that are redeemable across a variety of portals for equivalent money.

- Cross-enterprise platforms like PayBack, VISA, MASTERCARD facilitate value transfers across merchant establishments.

All the above cases can also be replayed on Blockchain platforms.

LIBRA coin is akin to an Amazon Pay balance point, issued on LIBRA Blockchain that operates on a decentralized and distributed network managed by a group of world's leading organizations of which Facebook is one. JPM Coin is administered over a Distributed Ledger and is used for inter-bank settlements within a closed network of banks.

The decentralized and distributed ledger nature of the LIBRA Blockchain offers a new paradigm of security and pseudonymity while having an additional advantage of minimizing the transaction costs and accountability in case of loss due to the accountability that goes with Permissioned Public Blockchain platforms.

Further, the LIBRA coin has an added advantage of being accepted in exchange for LIBRA coins, thus acting like an interoperable VISA system, with an added advantage of being operated with the safety net of Blockchain acting like a TTP. (Trusted Third Party)

Comparison between Centralised & Decentralised Asset coins		
Type of value exchange unit	Centralised Banking & Marketplace systems	Blockchain based decentralised systems
National Currency	Indian Rupee	Central Bank Digital Currency over a DLT
Global Currency	US Dollar	Bitcoin
Marketplace Token	Amazon Paybalance	LIBRA coin
Closed loop Merchant token	Mall Food court cash card	DAPP Token

Table 3.1 Comparison Between Centralized and Decentralized Asset Coins.

Currently, the US Dollar is seen as the globally interoperable currency accepted by most nations. In the recent past, several countries are experimenting with the concept of leveraging the internet for speedy transfer of value considering the impending proliferation of IOT & Industrial IOT-led Home automation, Industrial automation and Smart City projects across the world. There has been a strong need felt for a digital equivalent of the national currencies giving rise to the concept of Central bank digital currency (CBDC), also called digital fiat currency (a currency established as money by Government regulation or law). Central Bank Digital Currency is different from virtual currency and cryptocurrency, which are not issued by the state and lack the legal tender status declared by the Government.

Various countries are already experimenting with the concept of CBDC and it is considered a transitory step to the ultimate eventuality of a fully digitized currency with the added security measure offered by a Blockchain approach.

According to the BIS, today some 70% of central banks are looking at CBDC, with most of them considering Blockchain as the underlying technology.

Some of the global Distributed Ledger Technology-based CBDC projects disclosed in the public domain are given in the following table published by Bank of Thailand in their project report on the state of CBDC project being experimented by BOT in conjunction with R3 Corda, Indian IT major Wipro and several transnational banks.

Phase	Paper Published	Project Focus	DLT Platform Used
Bank of Canada		**Project Jasper**	
Phase 1	Mar. 2016	1. Create a wholesale interbank RTGS proof-of-concept on DLT Ethereum platform 2. Evaluate PFMIs against tokenised interbank payments	Ethereum
Phase 2	Dec. 2016	1. Rebuild original proof-of-concept on Corda 2. Build additional functionalities such as LSM	Corda
Phase 3	Oct. 2018	1. Integrate a liquidity savings mechanism for netting transactions 2. Examine DvP solutions for security settlement	Corda
Monetary Authority of Singapore		**Project Ubin**	
Phase 1	Aug. 2016	1. Build a proof-of-concept for domestic RTGS on a private Ethereum network 2. Identify the non-technical implications of moving this into a production environment 3. Integrate DLT with existing RTGS in a test environment to automate tokenisation and detokenisation	Ethereum
Phase 2	Jul. 2017	1. Expand on the original proof-of-concept by incorporating LSMs 2. Understand how RTGS privacy can be ensured on DLT 3. Compare alternative DLT platforms	Quorum, Corda, Hyperledger Fabric
Phase 3	Nov. 2018	1. Explore different combinations of DLT for DvP between cash and Singapore government bonds 2. Test and examine solutions designed by Anquan Capital, Deloitte, and Nasdaq	Ethereum, Hyperledger Fabric, Chain, Quorum, Anquan
Central Bank of Brazil			
Phase 1	Aug. 2016	1. Identify use cases and build a working prototype for the central bank using DLT 2. Identify realistic functionality and build a minimum proof-of-concept for RTGS system on DLT platform	Ethereum
Phase 2	Nov. 2016	1. Analyse competing blockchain platforms using the selected use case as a benchmark 2. Address the privacy issues identified in the previous phase	Corda
European Central Bank & Bank of Japan		**Project Stella**	
Phase 1	May 2017	1. Build RTGS system on DLT, including LSM functions 2. Assess safety and efficiency of current system in DLT implementation	Hyperledger Fabric
Phase 2	Nov. 2017	1. Build DvP proof-of-concept on different DLT platforms 2. Identify the trade-off between network size and performance 3. Assess DLT capability for cross-chain securities settlement	Quorum, Corda, Hyperledger Fabric, Elements
Hong Kong Monetary Authority		**Project Lionrock**	
Phase 1	Aug. 2016	1. Identify use cases and build a working prototype for the central bank using DLT 2. Identify realistic functionality and build a minimum proof of concept for RTGS system on DLT platform	Corda
South African Reserve Bank		**Project Khokha**	
Phase 1	Feb. 2018	1. Build an RTGS proof-of-concept on DLT, exploring on privacy and scalability 2. Perform tests under a variety of deployment models in different locations 3. Assess a Quorum-based interbank payment system	Quorum

Fig 3.17 Blockchain based CBDC projects across the world https://www.bot.or.th/English/FinancialMarkets/ProjectInthanon/Documents/Inthanon_Phase1_Report.pdf

Case Study: Central Bank Digital Currency experiment by Bank of Thailand (Project Inathon)

https://www.bot.or.th/English/FinancialMarkets/ProjectInthanon/Documents/Inthanon_Phase2_Report.pdf

Project Inthanon was devided into three progressive phases, each leveraging on the findings and learnings of the previous phase:

01 Phase 1 – Building the Fundamental

A POC for a DLT-based RTGS using wholesale CBDC for interbank settlement was built. A key highlight was the development of an innovative GR architecture with integrated Automated Liquidity Provision (ALP) functionality that achieved privacy and atomicity properties.

02 Phase 2 – Enhancing Functionalities

The objective is to build on the Phase 1 POC and augment it with additional functions to handle DvP settlement for interbank bond repo & trading, data reconciliation and handling of NR regulatory requirements. Outcomes from Phase 2 demonstrate the practicality of DLT at enabling transformative process improvement and technical feasibility of achieving DvP in real-time through an experimental MLSM.

03 Phase 3 – Exploring Cross-Border Funds Transfer Models

The DLT-based RTGS prototype will be expanded to connect with the other systems to support cross-border funds transfer transactions. The scope will also cover the regulatory and compliance issues from both THB and foreign currencies.

Fig 3.18

Bank of Thailand completed Phase-1 and Phase-2 successfully and has demonstrated many advantages of issuing the Central Bank-backed digital currencies over a Distributed ledger.

The findings from Phase-2 demonstrated the feasibility of Smart Contract utilization to automate bond life cycle events and DvP of inter-bank bond trading and repo transactions. The effective use of Smart Contracts has shown the potential to significantly streamline operational workflows and increase efficiencies. Fraud-prevention capabilities of the RTGS system were also augmented by the creation of a new end-to-end workflow that allowed validation of transactional information with external sources through integration points. The use of Smart Contracts for regulatory compliance purposes was also successfully tested in Phase-2 with the introduction of the NRFS mechanism, which could potentially eliminate multiple manual operational processes and allow banks to monitor NRBA/NRBS limits more effectively.

3.9 How the ICT-MAAFIAA Can Help

For a sound Blockchain consortium, the permanence of the platform, impeccable credentials, fair and impartially foolproof governance with utmost trust is the most important attribute. This can be provided by a Government – or United Nations-backed Permissioned Blockchain. Alternately, it should be backed by a collection of the most reputed and valuable organizations. We cannot have a more valuable and credible group than the ICT-MAAFIAA discussed earlier that do back such an infrastructure.

A consortium backed by leading players like the ICT – MAAFIAA we discussed could well be a possibility in the none-too-distant future giving rise to the following scenario:

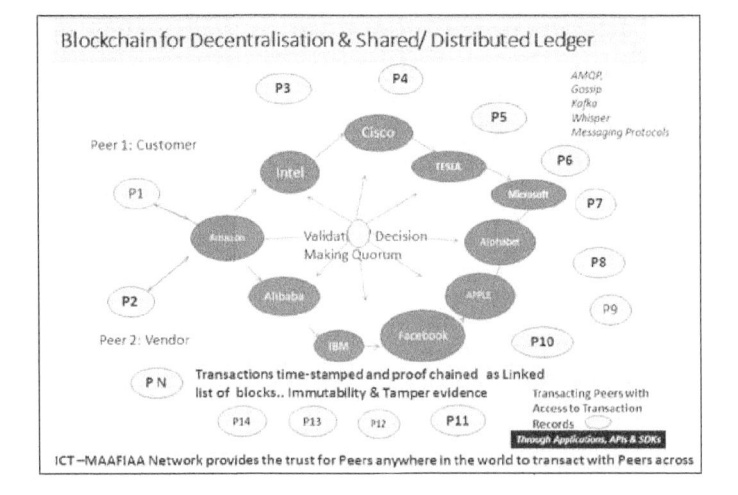

Fig 3.19 Blockchain for Decentralisation & Shared/ Distributed Ledger.

3.10 Blockchain 0–10

The value proposition of Blockchain and the various key concepts can well be summarized in the following manner with a table of count from 0–10. These concepts summarize the many points we are covering across the book in appropriate contexts.

0. Single Points of Failure elimination to de-risk against cyber-attacks

1. Single Source of Truth for multiple transacting parties

2. Non-Trusting Parties can use Blockchain as a Trust Anchor instead of Humans— prevention of double-spending

3. Triple Entry-Accounting with an indisputable and incorruptible record for tamper evidence

4. Key concepts for Business Blockchain: Shared ledger, Privacy, Smart Contracts, Consensus

5. Elements of Blockchain as per Gartner Framework: Encryption, Immutability, Tokenization, Decentralization, Distribution

6. Key application areas: Identity, Asset Provenance, Payments, Marketplace, Tokenization, Authenticity

7. DID benefits: Inclusion, Personalized engagement, Seamless Travel, Age and personal detail verification, Background checks, digital payments, One-click on-boarding

8. Consensus, Cooperation, Collaboration, Coordination, Cryptography (hashing, DSA, PKI, etc.), Confidentiality, Consortium, CBDC

9. Identity, Integration, Interoperability, Interchain, Intrachain, Interchange, Initiate (Pay), Immutability, Intermediate removal

10. Step Methodology for Determining Blockchain Use case

3.11 Welcome to a World of HOPE

Recently the world is witness to the uproar raised due to the failure on the part of Facebook to prevent the protection of identities of its members in the Cambridge Analytica case. In such a scenario, what then are the alternatives for global corporate citizens to express themselves freely and be connected across the world?

But then there is hope. The onset of the Artificial Intelligence empowered mammoth organizations with unlimited power, but with a single source of failure due to threats of cyber warfare, Ransomware and unscrupulous promoters have led to the people embracing Blockchain as a religion across the world. Blockchain has now given an unprecedented option for all peers across the world to be connected in a pseudonymous manner.

This is now leading to a movement that is going to take strength in the future as Blockchain paradigm cuts across the various sections of the world with a versatile, empowered and ubiquitous ecosystem. The conventional social media will no more be the preferred choice of communication.

The implementation of Blockchain-enabled KYC and self-sovereign identity will empower the citizens across the world to own their own data and use the various platforms designed for specific purposes in a safe and secure way while monetizing their activities.

The data in the Blockchain-enabled future will put the power back into the hands of the individuals. The identities of the world's citizens will be protected by Blockchain as they operate in a pseudonymous manner with metadata visible to the advertisers and platforms.

They can give permission to the platforms and data consumers, while they get paid for the same as well as their social media contributions. Several Blockchain-enabled platforms are already catching and the same are listed in the book *Blockchain the Untold Story*, which examines the Blockchain technology in all its earnest for the benefit of a safe and secure future for global citizens. (https://www.

amazon.in/Blockchain-untold-story-Srinivas-Mahankali-ebook/dp/B07GF6VL13/)

Welcome to a world of 'Hope' and empowerment-facilitating by this amazing paradigm of our era, Blockchain!

The excitement to adopt this new paradigm can be visualized by the amount of activity that is taking place across the world from Companies, Consortia and Countries including the European Union and the United Nations.

3.12 Companies Consortia and Countries Catalyzing the Blockchain World—Some of the World's Leading Blockchain Consortia are given below

1. Enterprise Ethereum Alliance (https://entethalliance.org/)

The EEA is a member-led no-profit industry consortium consisting of over 150 organizations to work around the adoption of Ethereum Blockchain technology as an open-standard to empower enterprises working for a decentralized world across various use cases for Government and enterprises. It comprises global leading organizations including ConsenSys, CME Group, Cornell University's research group, Toyota Research Institute, Samsung SDS, Microsoft, Intel, J. P. Morgan, Cooley LLP, Merck KGaA, DTCC, Deloitte, Accenture, Banco Santander, BNY Mellon, ING, National Bank of Canada MasterCard, Cisco Systems, Sberbank and Scotiabank.

2. Hyperledger (https://www.hyperledger.org/)

Hyperledger (or the Hyperledger project) is a cross-sectoral umbrella project of open-source Blockchains and related tools, started in December 2015 by the Linux Foundation,[1] and has received contributions from IBM, Intel and SAP Ariba, to support the collaborative development of Blockchain-based distributed ledgers. Global leaders across various domains like Technology platforms, Blockchain platforms, System integrators, Management consultancies, Financial services, Manufacturing and Supply Chain organizations collaborate as part of the Hyperledger foundation on various solutions for different applications.

3. R3 (https://www.r3.com/) led consortium

R3 (R3 LLC) is a New York-based Enterprise Blockchain technology company leading an ecosystem of more than 300 firms working together to build distributed applications on top of Corda (known as CorDapps) for usage across industries such as financial services, insurance, healthcare, trade finance, and digital assets. Corda, an open-sourced Distributed Ledger Platform records, manages and synchronizes financial agreements and standardizes data and business processes.

4. TradeLens https://www.tradelens.com

TradeLens, jointly developed by IBM and Maersk GTD is an open and neutral Blockchain platform serving the ecosystem of the supply chain in information sharing and collaboration across the value chain, thereby increasing industry innovation, reducing trade friction and ultimately promoting more global trade.

5. IBM Food Trust: https://www.ibm.com/in-en/ Blockchain/solutions/food-trust

IBM Food Trust is a consortium of producers, suppliers, manufacturers, retailers and any other business serving the global food supply chain with a focus to create a trusted, transparent, safer and efficient food system across the world. Walmart is one of the key members of the consortium along with IBM.

6. MediLedger: https://www.mediledger.com

The MediLedger project is a collaboration between Chronicled and The LinkLab, connecting leading pharmaceutical manufacturers and distributors to explore Blockchain technologies by bringing together expertise in both pharmaceutical supply chain and Blockchain technologies. The project is building an industry-owned Permissioned Blockchain network for the pharmaceutical sector based on open standards and specifications. Network nodes are set to be distributed among and operated by industry participants and technology providers who serve the industry with an aim to meet compliance and regulatory requirements of the industry, provide Track-and-Trace for the products and eliminate the role of fake drugs and also to enable the parties for easy mutual reconciliation of accounts.

7. Trusted IOT Alliance: https://www.iiconsortium.org

The Trusted IOT Alliance is an open-source software foundation with a mission—to leverage the power of Blockchain and Distributed Ledger Technologies. It consists of leading IOT companies in the world who are together working to unravel the disruptive power of all emerging technologies. It is now consolidated with The Industrial Internet Consortium, a global not-for-profit partnership of Industry, Government and Academia.

8. MOBI: https://dlt.mobi

The Mobility Open Blockchain Initiative is a consortium formed by global automobile sector majors across the world to leverage Blockchain technologies for safer and greener automation-powered transportation technologies. Almost all the Fortune 500 members from the automobile technology, vehicle and ancillary manufacturing, consultancy and services space are members of the consortium.

9. B3I: https://b3i.tech/home.html

B3I is an insurance industry consortium and comprises of over 20 insurance majors and 20 customers and service providers. The consortium is focusing on leveraging Blockchain to improve coordination among the players and eliminate fraud. It is working on developing standards, protocols and network infrastructure to remove friction in risk transfer and give end consumers of insurance better and faster access to insurance.

10. Synaptic Health Alliance (https://www.synaptichealthalliance.com/)

Synaptic Health Alliance is a consortium of health care majors like Aetna, Humana, MultiPlan, Optum, Quest Diagnostics, and United Healthcare. It is working to leverage Blockchain to tackle the problems associated with data duplication across multiple silos that involve feeding activities such as claims processing, payment integrity processes, provider and member attribution, provider directories, and more.

11. Global Shipping Business Network: https://www.cargosmart.ai/en

GSBN is a global consortium of leading global shipping organizations and port operators formed to leverage the power of emerging technologies, especially Blockchain for smooth cargo transportation through seamless documentation, consignment traceability and financial transactions including support to Trade Finance activities. The members include industry-leading ocean carriers and terminal operators, namely CMA CGM, COSCO SHIPPING LINES, COSCO SHIPPING Ports, Hapag-Lloyd, Hutchison Ports, OOCL, Port of Qingdao, PSA International, and Shanghai International Port Group (SIPG),

There are many such leading consortia as mentioned in the table providing the list of Blockchain consortia and this is a growing trend that promises to catalyze the migration of all enterprises in every sector to leverage Blockchain for collaboration for seamless service to customers and increased productivity.

The Governance of the Consortia needs to be fair, transparent and democratic. In future, the consortia will be leading providers of jobs across the emerging technology space unlike today's centralized organizations like ICT-MAAFIAA mentioned earlier and this is the new paradigm, all professionals should get adapted to.

Companies implementing Blockchain-based Decentralized Applications

Ant Financials' Blockchain solution (Alibaba):

Kaola, the e-commerce platform owned by the global e-commerce giant, Alibaba, has integrated Blockchain in its cross-border supply chain management system to help with traceability and product data reconciliation. It also leverages Blockchain for improving the liquidity of traders and manufacturers using the platform by enabling them to get quick loans through Supplier Financing.

Anthem:

Health insurance giant Anthem offers Blockchain-based health records management for its millions of customers to securely store and share their personal electronic health records.

Brave: https://brave.com/features

Built by the Brendan Eich, inventor of JavaScript and the founder of Mozilla, Brave browser offers a decentralized web browser with revolutionary benefits. It empowers the surfers with extreme privacy, not storing the data unless opted for promotions and provides an opportunity to earn rewards by viewing advertisements. It aims to be a leader in Blockchain applications for digital marketing and advertisement networks.

Chainlink https://chain.link

Chainlink offers very useful middleware for integrating Blockchain Smart Contracts securely to the external world to sources of data, APIs and Payment gateways. In contrast to centralized oracles that provide the inputs to Smart Contracts with the possibility of a Single Point of Failure, Chainlink offers a decentralized approach to offer the Blockchain's distributed approach for enhanced dependability and security as well. More details can be read from https://link.smartcontract.com/whitepaper.

Chain of Origin (Amazon):

Amazon's Blockchain solution for Supply Chain tracking offers its clients the ability to track their products from the source destination.

China Construction Bank: CCB is leveraging Blockchain across several projects like Supply chain provenance, Government grant utilization tracking, Carbon credit trading, cross-border e-commerce settlements, etc.

CipherTrace: https://ciphertrace.com

CipherTrace is an analytics platform for risk management in the Blockchain industry. It helps in detecting money laundering, powers law enforcement investigations, and enables regulatory supervision. It enables regulators to trace criminal activities like the laundering of over 100 Million US Dollars' worth of Cryptocurrency by North Korean actors. https://www.justice.gov/opa/pr/two-chinese-nationals-charged-laundering-over-100-million-cryptocurrency-exchange-hack.

Cipher: (https://avanzainnovations.com/Blockchain/)

Cipher is an exciting middleware that facilitates Blockchain orchestration and governance by building interoperability across all these underlying technologies while ensuring application integrity and performance—regardless of versioning, governance, etc. issues. It helps move silo-based structures into a more refined interconnected solution on the Blockchain. It acts as reconciliation and network across multiple-siloed systems and has enabled Smart Dubai Government in extensive digitization and elimination of huge wastage of resources used for reconciliation.

Daimler:

Daimler is leveraging Blockchain for digitally tracking contracts across its group companies and divisions. It is also working on facilitating cash settlements across its partners, employees, vehicle drivers and their vendors like petrol bunks and other vendors.

DLT.SG https://www.dlt.sg

DltLedgers empowers global supply chain and e-commerce platforms to be a part of the global network and leverage the power of Blockchain for a variety of next-generation applications like end-to-end traceability, integrate with the finance partners for trade finance, establish product provenance for eliminating fakes facilitating trust for the respective customers. DLT ledgers facilitate integration with legacy ERP systems like SAP through APIs. Origin Trail (https://origintrail.io/), EverLedger https://www.everledger.io/are some of the leading Blockchain-based decentralized applications enabling transparent Supply Chains globally.

DTCC (Depository Trust and Clearing Corporation)

The global leader and industry-owned post-trade settlement company, US-based DTCC is working on revamping its Trade information Warehouse and move the post-trade settlement process lifecycle onto a Distributed Ledger Platform powered by DLT firm, AXONI, to reduce costs and increase efficiencies in the post-trade process."

Facebook:

Based on a technology derived from VMWare's Hotstuff, Facebook has launched the LIBRA Blockchain platform, as a part of a global consortium to issue and track an asset-backed Cryptocurrency LIBRA coin on a Permission Blockchain platform. This is seen as an important transition step toward a decentralized world that will see the consumers across the world conducting their e-commerce and social media transactions on a decentralized and distributed Blockchain platform in due course.

GE Aviation:

General Electric's Aviation Company leverages Blockchain for its supply chain and for tracking the part provenance for the entire automobile and aviation spare parts and airplane engines it produces through its solution 'back-to-birth' aircraft maintenance record.

HSBC:

World's leading Bank, HSBC has leveraged Blockchain for multiple applications like conducting trillions of US Dollars of transactions on its Blockchain platform, FX everywhere, issuing Letter of Credits for the large clients and storing Billions of US Dollars' worth of securities in its digital vault secured by Blockchain.

JP Morgan and Signature Bank:

Global banking giant JP Morgan launched a Blockchain network, 'Inter-Bank information Network,' (IIN), where it connects over 100 banks to undertake inter-bank remittances using JPM Coin, a Blockchain-powered stable coin that facilitates instant settlements across the branches anywhere in the world. Similarly, New York-based, FDIC-insured Signature Bank launched Signet coin on Ethereum Blockchain for lighting fast settlements in cross-border transactions.

KYC-Chain: https://kyc-chain.com/

KYC-Chain is a Blockchain-based all-in-one workflow solution for enterprises to verify your customers' identities, streamline the KYC on-boarding process and manage the entire customer lifecycle with database verification with access to documents and details spanning 240 countries. It enables enterprises to wade through the complex set of regulations connected with data protection and remain compliant to GDPR, KYC, AML, CRS, MIFID and FACTA laws globally.

Mastercard:

The global credit card major is leveraging its vast network across the e-commerce and banking circles to launch supply chain financing and cross-border remittance solutions in partnership with the R3 Corda platform.

Microsoft:

Microsoft offers the Azure Blockchain Tokenization platform and Azure Blockchain service to enable its clients to tokenize physical assets on a Blockchain and manage them effectively in the platform. Azure's Blockchain data manager enables the organizations to integrate Blockchain data into their existing applications in a seamless manner. This feature has got a great potential to ease many of the challenges faced by existing Blockchain applications w.r.t interoperability and integration in a disparate multi-enterprise scenario.

Tencent:

Tencent, the global leader in the internet and parent company of WeChat is working on a Blockchain platform to provide a single source of truth to employees of all organizations by enabling Blockchain-enabled digital billing and settlements.

Tracr (DeBeers) and Everledger:

Tracr and Everledger record the diamonds from the time they are mined till their entire lifespan along with the details of the mining conditions, finest details and nuances of design and the ownership changes at every level. This will ensure that the supply chains are free of inhuman exploitations and offer the possibility to trace the ownerships when stolen diamonds are presented for sale anywhere.

TraceDonate: https://www.tracedonate.com

TraceDonate is a donation platform powered by Blockchain technology that offers end-to-end transparency.

Charitable activities often suffer from the lack of trust for the donors about the credentials of the charity providers and the execution of the programs. The donors may not be able to get a clear view of the utilization of the money they donate. TraceDonate connects the donors, charitable institutions like international NGOs, implementers and the receivers on a Distributed ledger and offers them complete traceability of the charitable activity from the time a donation is received, till it reaches its desired utilization through a digital identity and verification program.

Trust Your Supplier: https://www.trustyoursupplier.com

IBM and Blockchain services company Chainyard joined forces with world's leading organizations like Anheuser-Busch InBev, Cisco, GlaxoSmithKline, Lenovo, Nokia, Schneider Electric and Vodafone, BHP, etc., launched a global consortium-based Permissioned Blockchain platform for seamless on-boarding of suppliers across supply chains with a standardized verification of credentials, acting as a Single Source of Truth. This vastly benefits the procurement processes of large companies by eliminating duplications of efforts and potential vendor-related frauds for a nominal cost and makes possible tracking the supplier information across their lifecycle on a Distributed ledger.

Leading countries working on Blockchain

"Trust, but verify" is a rhyming Russian proverb, used by Former USA President Ronald Reagan in the context of nuclear disarmament discussions with the Soviet Union.

Blockchain with its ability to act as a Trust Anchor and provide an auditable track record closely symbolizes this mantra. Many Governments across the world are exploring/leveraging Blockchain to offer transparent, efficient and cost-effective services to their citizens and industry. The following are some of the noted efforts by Governments across the world.

1. **Brazil** is using Blockchain-based Government e-Procurement to put a check on corruption in all Government purchases. Online Bid Solution, a Blockchain-based platform tracks the process of public biddings for Government projects and purchase processes between various co-operative societies and industry bodies.

2. **China** is leveraging Blockchain to fight corruption and disintermediate tax collections. China's Government is launching its digital currency powered by Permissioned DLT and facilitate the Public Blockchain ecosystem in a big way. Leading companies like Alibaba, Tencent and thousands of other companies are working on implementing Blockchain projects across every possible use case, spurring innovation and efficiency to a new plane.

3. **Dubai** is patronizing Blockchain to eliminate all paper records across its governance, land records management, Police evidence tracking, Passport and VISA tracking, Cross/border remittances,

Citizen Medical records tracking, etc., and save 5.5 billion dirhams annually in document processing alone—equal to the one Burj Khalifa's worth of value every year.

4. **Estonia** is extensively using Blockchain for the Integrity of data pertaining to all public and citizen records, Critical Infrastructure Protection and Secured access of all Government services to citizens through a Blockchain-enabled digital identity.

5. **European Union:** European Blockchain services infrastructure project, EBSI, was launched by the European Union enables users to store and transmit data in a secure, decentralized manner and deliver better services to Europe's citizens.

6. **India's Telecom Regulatory Authority** is using Distributed Ledger Technology for tracking Unsolicited Commercial. Communication. Several states, Ministries, Income Tax department, Customs department, Public Sector Undertakings, NPCI and Police departments are vigorously exploring Blockchain to improve transparency, efficiency and eliminate corruption and fake products, documents, identity and certificates menace.

7. **Singapore** is working on a Blockchain-based payment system using digital Singapore Dollars, that can be used to execute inter-bank and cross-currency remittances quickly and affordably and with fewer intermediaries. Being a global hub for Finance and Supply Chain activities and organizations, Singapore Government enables

a vibrant Blockchain ecosystem for enterprises to experiment and implement entire spectrum of Permissioned and Permissionless Blockchain applications across Finance, Supply Chain, trade finance, Crowdfunding, health insurance, Digital SGD, Academic certificates, etc.

8. **Uganda** is leveraging Blockchain in its Pharma Supply Chain to fight fake drug menace by eliminating them.

9. **UK** Government has been exploring Blockchain for several use cases like Central Bank Digital Currency for instant Inter-bank remittances, clearing and settlement, land records management, Government Data Provenance, Voting, Benefit and Charity distribution and Food safety in Supply Chains.

10. **USA:** US Government is working extensively on several Blockchain projects in Pharmaceuticals, Food, Cannabis, Defense Supply Chain provenance, health record tracking, Clinical records management, etc. Department of Homeland Security is researching Blockchain extensively for Critical Infrastructure protection using Blockchain-enabled identification systems.

4

PROJECTS, POSSIBILITIES, PROBLEMS

Provenance, Authenticity, Trust and Sustained Development

4.1 Blockchain-based Application Patterns and Architecture

Blockchain is, in essence, a data structure of an ordered list of blocks. Every block in the Blockchain is "chained" to the previous block, using a hashed value of the previous block. The security features of the hash function prevent the alteration of transactions on the Blockchain without invalidating the chain of hashes. This design includes computational constraints and consensus protocols applied to the creation of blocks to prevent tampering of the information on the Blockchain.

It is only imperative that such an immutable Distributed ledger will find its applications ranging from finance to a decentralized internet. The architecture of a software system, where Blockchain is one of the components is such that the Blockchain acts as an alternative for storing and sharing data, as well as executing Smart Contracts. The Blockchain component might also have tokens as digital currencies or representing other assets. The privacy and scalability limitations of Blockchain deem auxiliary databases in the system useful.

The external world and traditional systems interact with Blockchain applications through a Blockchain Proxy layer connected to the platform. Blockchain Proxy layer abstracts many complexities associated with the interaction between disparate paradigms. It has the following main utilities.

1. Simple, convenient and familiar interface for interaction to push transactions and check outputs

2. Provide access and service visibility as per functionality envisaged and permissions built-in

3. Provide integration points with internal enterprise systems and between other external systems, oracles and other Blockchain systems through APIs and data connector middleware

4. Communicate real-time updates to Blockchain ledger to the participants

5. Provide an events-exchange-mechanism to update systems and databases in and out of the Blockchain platform as envisaged

Blockchain is especially suitable for inter-enterprise or multiparty applications. Hence the most suitable model for implementing a Blockchain application is a democratic and collaborative approach of multiparty, Multi-Enterprise cooperation, coordination and collaborations.

While undertaking Blockchain projects, the following activities need to be considered:

- Prioritize problems
- Select the most appropriate platform

- Undertake POCs, Implement Pilots and scale successful pilots. Re-engineer and align internal processes for Blockchain implementation

- Undertake step-by-step implementation of the entire Blockchain-based system to

    a. Derive incremental benefits through integrating with back-end organizations, ERP and other systems

    b. Expand the scope to derive more efficiencies through increased involvement of employees at various levels and by increasing cross-enterprise network strength and collaboration

    c. Leverage increased network strength for expanding collaboration across many facets and offering more services as well as superior facilities to customers and other partners

    d. Deriving the benefits of efficiencies as envisaged by the Distributed Ledger Technology and increased Trust offered by the Blockchain system.

A fair and professional Trust Anchor that offers fair and transparent management, a powerful Blockchain platform with durable secured storage, accessible to all participants via open APIs through a set of open standards to all participants for exchanging information and offering an open application and services marketplace are some of the topmost requirements of implementing a successful Blockchain consortium.

Though typically a large organization or an industry association and a technology provider join hands to start working on a Blockchain implementation with foresight, over a period of time, a consortium will be formed and a new entity will come into place, like the United Nations Organization that is governed in an utmost professional manner.

A typical architecture of a Consortium Blockchain implementation is given below:

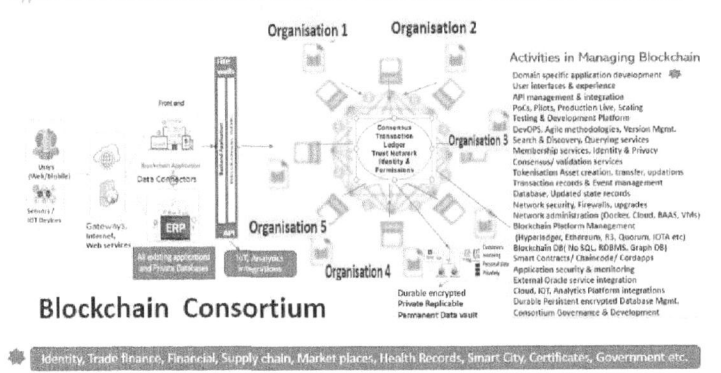

Fig 4.1 A typical Architecture for Blockchain Governance and Activities for Consortium Orchestration.

Collection of common Blockchain Application Architecture patterns

Blockchain has many versatile use cases, and most of them can require relatively few patterns to implement. The Blockchain-based application pattern collection includes 15 design patterns that shape the architectural elements and their interactions in Blockchain-based applications. These patterns are so devised as to align the application with the unique properties of Blockchain, curb its limitations, and achieve other quality attributes.

These patterns can be segregated based on the fundamental needs they fulfill.

- The patterns about the **interaction between Blockchain and the external world** describe different ways for Blockchain to communicate data with the external world, including *Verifier*, *Reverse Verifier,* and *Legal and Smart Contract pair.*

- The **data management patterns** are about managing data on and off-Blockchain, including *Encrypting on-chain data*, *Tokenization*, *Off-chain data storage*, and *State channel*.

- The **security patterns** deal with the security aspect of the Blockchain-based application and aim to add dynamism to the authorization of transactions and smart contracts. They comprise of multiple *authorizations*, *Off-chain secret-enabled dynamic authorization* and *X-confirmation*.

- The **contract structural patterns** define the dependencies among Smart Contracts and the immutable behavior of Smart Contracts. They aid in overcoming the primary challenge, which hinders the evolution of Blockchain-based applications: *How to upgrade a Smart Contract to a new version?* **Contract registry** and ***data contract*** are two patterns that target to improve the upgradability of Smart Contracts. **Embedded permission** and **Factory contract** are patterns that aim to improve the security of Smart Contracts. Finally, **Incentive execution** concerns *the maintenance of Smart Contracts.*

The pattern collection provides architectural guidance for developers to build applications on the Blockchain. Some patterns are designed specifically for applications keeping in mind the unique properties of the Blockchain. Others are variants of existing software patterns applied to Smart Contracts. Let us delve deeper into the Blockchain-based application pattern collection by examining the patterns of how they uniquely solve different types of problems.

A more detailed explanation of these concepts is beyond the scope of this book and can be referred from the white paper written by Xiwei Xu, Cesare Pautasso, Liming Zhu, Qinghua Lu, and Ingo Weber. 2018. (A Pattern Collection for Blockchain-based Applications. 1,1(May2018),33pages). https://www.researchgate.net/ publication/325439030_A_Pattern_Collection_for_ Blockchain-based_Applications/

Interaction with external world patterns

The primary architectural consideration for a Blockchain-based application is to decide what data and Smart Contracts should be kept on and off-chain while bearing performance and privacy concerns in mind.

Verifier

As the Blockchain is increasingly being used as a distributed database for more general purposes other than financial services, the application might need to interact with other external systems. So, the validation of transactions on the Blockchain might depend on states of external systems.

PROBLEM: The execution environment of a Blockchain is self-contained and can only access information present in the data and transactions present on the Blockchain. Besides, the state of external systems is not directly accessible to Smart Contracts.

SOLUTION: A verifier is a Trusted Third Party introduced to evaluate conditions that cannot be expressed in a Smart Contract running within the Blockchain environment and thereby connect this closed execution environment with the external world. In essence, it provides Smart Contracts with information about the external world. The verifier can be implemented both inside a Blockchain network as well as a server outside the Blockchain. All in all, the verifier boosts *connectivity*, *enhances trust* in an unbiased third party, and *checks validity* within the network.

Reverse Verifier

In a software system where Blockchain is one of the components, the other parts might need the data stored and Smart Contracts running on the Blockchain to check certain conditions. The Reverse Verifier relies on Smart Contracts running on Blockchain to validate data and check the required status.

PROBLEM: Certain domains use exceedingly large and mature systems that comply with standards by default. The need of the hour then is a non-intrusive approach to leverage the existing systems with Blockchain without changing its core.

SOLUTION: The ID of the transactions or blocks on the Blockchain is data that can be integrated into the existing systems with ease. Smart contracts running on the Blockchain can implement the validation of said data. The Reverse Verifier pattern boosts *connectivity* while employing a *non-intrusive* approach toward existing systems.

Legal and Smart Contract Pair

With the digitization of the legal industry, digital signatures have found its way to signing legal agreements. Digital legal agreements need to be executed and enforced without losing the value of the legal prose.

PROBLEM: An independent, trustworthy execution platform trusted by the involved participants is needed to execute the digital legal agreement. Blockchain, bound with corresponding Smart Contracts, is an ideal candidate.

SOLUTION: The Smart Contract implements conditions defined in the legal agreement and, when deployed, possesses a variable to store the hash-value of the legal agreement. This bidirectional binding of a physical agreement with a Smart Contract establishes the bridge between the off-chain physical agreement and the on-chain Smart Contract. This pairing automates the *enforcement of legal conditions* and creates an *audit trail*. But it does so by lowering *expressiveness*, *enforceability*, and *interpretation of legal terms*.

Data Management Patterns

Encrypting On-Chain Data

For some applications on the Blockchain, there might be commercially critical data that should only be accessible to the involved participants. The confidentiality of such data should be ensured by encrypting it and making it inaccessible to the other users.

PROBLEM: Data Privacy is compromised because all the information on the Blockchain is publicly available to its participants. There is no privileged user within the Blockchain network, no matter the type of Blockchain: public, consortium, or private.

Solution: To preserve the participants' privacy, their data should be encrypted before insertion into the Blockchain. A possible design for sharing encrypted data among multiple participants is by utilizing a secret key. One of the involved participants creates a secret key for encrypting data and distributes it. When a participant needs to add a new data item, they then encrypt it using the secret key. Only the participants allowed to access the transaction have the secret key and can decrypt the information. The benefit of this method is the fulfillment of the *confidentiality* needs of participants. But it also has its drawbacks—*compromised key*, *key sharing issues*, and *access revocation*.

Tokenization

Tokenization is a means to reduce risk in handling high-value financial instruments by replacing them with equivalents (Think of tokens in a casino). Tokens can represent a wide range of goods which are transferable and fungible.

Problem: Tokens representing assets should be the authoritative source of the corresponding assets.

Solution: Of the two ways to achieve Tokenization on the Blockchain, naive tokens on a Blockchain (e.g., BTC on Bitcoin, ETC on Ethereum) are part of a system where the tokens represent monetary value or physical assets. However, this method is limited because it can only implement the title transfer of the assets with limited conditions checking. A more flexible way is to define a data structure in a Smart Contract to represent physical assets. By using Smart Contracts, some functions can be implemented and associated with the ownership transfer. *Risk reduction* and *authority enforcement* are the pros of Tokenization. However, some levels of *integrity* and *standardization* are compromised.

Off-Chain Data Storage

Some applications consider using the Blockchain to guarantee the integrity of large amounts of data that may not fit in the Blockchain by employing hashing.

PROBLEM: The Blockchain has limited storage capacity, and storing large amounts of data within a transaction may be impossible due to the limited size of the blocks. On the other hand, data cannot take advantage of the immutability or integrity guarantees without being stored on the Blockchain.

SOLUTION: For large amounts of data, rather than storing the raw data directly on the Blockchain, a smaller representation of the data is stored instead. The solution is to store a hash-value of the raw data on-chain. A hash function like *SHA* generates the hash-value, which maps data of arbitrary size to data of fixed size. If even one bit of the data changes, its corresponding hash-value would change as well, thus guaranteeing the *integrity* of data and reducing the *cost of storage* in the Blockchain. However, some of the drawbacks include *data loss* and *data sharing*.

State Channel

Micro-payments are payments that can be as small as a few cents, and Blockchain has the potential to be used for such transactions. The question is the necessity and cost-effectiveness of storing all micro-payment transactions on the Blockchain.

PROBLEM: Transactions can take minutes to an hour to commit to the Blockchain. Due to the extended overhead and high transaction fees on a Public Blockchain, it is infeasible to store every micro-payment transaction on the Blockchain network.

SOLUTION: A payment channel can is established between two participants, with deposits from participants locked up as security in a contract during the channel's lifetime. The channel keeps the intermediate states of the micropayment off-chain and only stores the finalized payment on-chain. This system of channels can accentuate the *speed*, *throughput*, *privacy*, and reduce the *cost of transactions* and can compromise the *trustworthiness* of participants.

Security Patterns

Multiple Authorization

In Blockchain-based applications, activities require authorization by multiple Blockchain addresses. A set of Blockchain addresses that can authorize a transaction is pre-defined. But only its subset is needed to allow transactions.

PROBLEM: The actual addresses that authorize an activity can fluctuate with the availability of the authorities.

SOLUTION: A dynamic way is to decide upon the set of Blockchain addresses for authorization just before the corresponding transaction is committed to the Blockchain network. An M-of-N multi-signature method can define that M out of N private keys are required to authorize the transaction. Such an on-chain mechanism enables a more flexible binding of authorities. As *flexibility* and *tolerance of lost keys* come along with this method, it compromises knowledge of *pre-defined authorities* and the *cost of dynamism*.

Off-Chain Secret-Enabled Dynamic Authorization

In Blockchain-based applications, activities need to be authorized by one or more participants that may be unknown when a transaction is submitted.

Problem: Sometimes, the authority that can authorize a given activity is unknown when the corresponding transaction commits to the Blockchain. Blockchain also does not support dynamic binding with an address of a participant who is unknown in the particular transaction.

Solution: A single off-chain secret can enable dynamic authorization when the participant authorizing a transaction is unknown beforehand. With this solution, the recipient of the transaction does not need to be defined previously in the contract. The solution encourages *dynamism* and *interoperability*. But the secret is of *single-use* and requires protection against *loss of secrets*.

X-Confirmation

The immutability of a Blockchain using Proof-of-work consensus is probabilistic. There is always a chance that the most recent few blocks get replaced by a competing chain fork.

Problem: At the time a fork occurs, there is uncertainty as to which branches will remain in the Blockchain and which won't.

Solution: A security strategy is to wait for a certain number (X) of blocks to be generated after the transaction gets included in a block. After X blocks, the transaction gets committed onto the chain and perceived as immutable. The solution fortifies the *immutability* of transactions but may increase *latency*.

Contract structural patterns

Contract Registry

Like any software application, Blockchain-based applications should upgrade to new versions. These updates involve renewing the on-chain functions defined in Smart Contracts as well.

Problem: Smart contracts deployed on the Blockchain cannot upgrade because its code stored on the Blockchain is immutable.

Solution: An on-chain registry contract is used to maintain a mapping between user-defined names and the Blockchain addresses of the registered contracts. The address of the registry contract needs to be known off-chain. Before invoking the registered contact, the address of the latest version of a Smart Contract is identified by looking up its name on the contract registry. The solution provides *transparent upgradability* and *version control*. But it can detract the *extent of upgradability* and increase *costs*.

Data Contract

The need to upgrade a Blockchain-based application and its original Smart Contracts over time is ultimately necessary. Even as logic and data change at different times with different frequencies.

Problem: While upgrading Smart Contracts, the upgrading transactions might contain large data storage for copying the data from the old to the new Smart Contract, and porting data to newer versions might require multiple transactions.

Solution: To avoid movement of data during contract upgrades, the data store is isolated from the rest of the code. So, data in different Smart Contracts are isolated, and the more generic and flexible data structure is used by all the other logic Smart Contracts and is unlikely to require changes. The benefits include *upgradability* and *cost savings*.

Embedded Permission

The Smart Contracts running on Blockchain can be accessed by all the participants and other Smart Contracts by default because there are no privileged users. In the case of a Public Blockchain, particularly, every participant in the network can access the information and code stored on the Blockchain.

PROBLEM: A Smart Contract by default has no owner and once deployed, the author of the Smart Contract has no special privilege. A Permissionless function can be triggered by unauthorized users accidentally and can deem Blockchain-based applications vulnerable.

SOLUTION: By embedding permission-control to every Smart Contract function to check permissions for every caller that triggers the functions defined in the Smart Contract, access gets restricted to unauthorized users. Permission-control can enhance *security* and *authorization* of the Smart Contracts, the caveat being a *higher cost* of implementation of permission-control.

Factory Contract

Applications based on the Blockchain might need to use multiple instances of a standard contract with customization. Each contract instance is created by instantiating a contract template that can be stored off-chain in a code repository, or on-chain, within a Smart Contract.

PROBLEM: Keeping the contract template off-chain cannot guarantee consistency between different Smart Contract instances created from the same template because the template source code can be independently modified.

Solution: Smart contracts get created from a contract factory deployed on the Blockchain. The factory contract has its roots in the off-chain source code. The factory will then contain the definition of multiple Smart Contracts. This method provides boosted *security* and *efficiency* at the *cost of deployment* and *function calls*.

Incentive Execution

Smart contracts are event-driven programs that cannot execute autonomously. The functions defined in a Smart Contract need to be triggered either by an external transaction or another Smart Contract to execute.

Problem: Users of a Smart Contract have no direct benefit from calling the accessorial functions. When using a Public Blockchain, executing these functions cause extra monetary cost, leading up to an expensive process.

Solution: Providing rewards to the caller of the contract function for invoking the execution can guarantee the *completeness* of regular services through accessorial functions, the downside being the *unguaranteed execution* of accessory functions.

To conclude, Blockchain can be viewed holistically as a fundamental building block of large-scale decentralized software systems. Patterns that show how to make good use of the Blockchain in the design of systems and applications are imperative for the effective use of Blockchain to this end.

As Blockchain acts as a Trusted Third Party to record the transaction history between two parties, it becomes imperative for members to have secured and private access to their records without recourse to the other dominant party's (example Bank, Market place, etc.) or the creator of records. The Court of Justice of the European Union has mandated the Blockchain administrators to ensure the same in one of its judgments in January 2017. Hence, this needs to be ensured and a replicated encrypted database for Disaster Recovery and accessible to the clients. This is an opportunity for third party-regulated Data Vault providers.

4.2 Setting and Scaling Up Blockchain Projects

Blockchain defined as an Augmented Distributed Ledger Technology is very much valuable for streamlining inter-enterprise processes and by employing a new generation of applications known as Smart contracts, facilitates collaboration, coordination and collaboration through real-time communication between unknown peers across the world for trusted, secure and transparent transactions.

Being an inter-enterprise platform, it is not amenable for a variety of applications that are internal to the organization.

It is very imperative to put in place a common agenda for several ecosystem players and ensure that the 'Why Blockchain' and 'What is in it for me' part of the questions are convincingly put forth and demonstrated.

Gartner, a leading Technology & Management research advisory & consultancy in the world has outlined a three-phase approach to implementing Blockchain solutions across five different dimensions. The dimensions outlined by Gartner to describe a true Blockchain system are distribution, encryption, immutability, Tokenization and Decentralization.

Distribution implies sharing the ledger of transaction records across multiple parties of the system, across the globe.

Decentralization implies a collective decision-making and ensures no single person or entity control over the decisions and assets in the Blockchain system.

Immutability implies that the transactions cannot be reversed once approved and recorded on the ledger,

Encryption helps in secured access and authorization to participants for conducting transactions and authorization of transactions to ensure the intended parties as per access protocols recorded in the system are followed by using PKI based approaches, ECDSA algorithms to link public keys and private keys and usage of hashing for preserving data integrity, ZKP protocols for privacy protection, etc.

Tokenization results in the digitized representation of real-life assets, rights and identities on the Blockchain for tracking them through their lifetime.

The three Phases of implementation are described below:

- **Phase-1: Blockchain-inspired solutions:** These solutions involving a few but not all of the five elements described above are incremental in nature, mostly supplementing the existing business processes without causing any disruption or distraction. These are mostly centered around the creation of Proof of Concepts and Pilots to establish Proof of value and achieve incremental benefits for increased efficiencies and improvement of existing processes.

- **Phase-2: Blockchain-complete solutions:** Once the enterprises are confident about the value proposition of Blockchain applications, a gradual expansion of scope to complement existing processes, replace them with inter-enterprise collaborated processes for greater economies of scale and tremendous benefits to their customers will be implemented. During this phase, the scope also involves leveraging all the five elements mentioned earlier.

- **Phase-3: Enhanced-Blockchain solutions:** Involves combining different emerging technologies like Artificial intelligence, Machine learning, Internet of things with all the five elements of the Blockchain for integrated applications for autonomous agents, smart cities, supply chains, etc., for secured scaling and accelerated disruption.

Investments in Blockchain become viable when the size of the network increases and grows bigger and bigger so that the investments are amortized over a larger value of businesses generating increased savings.

4.3 Deciding on Blockchain Implementation

But before the need for Blockchain as a solution is decided upon, it is imperative to consider all other options to solve the problem in hand through traditional approaches. The following figure gives a list of questions that need to be answered, leading to the decision to implement Blockchain as a solution to solve the problems and provide a high Return-On-Investments.

Do You Need a Blockchain?

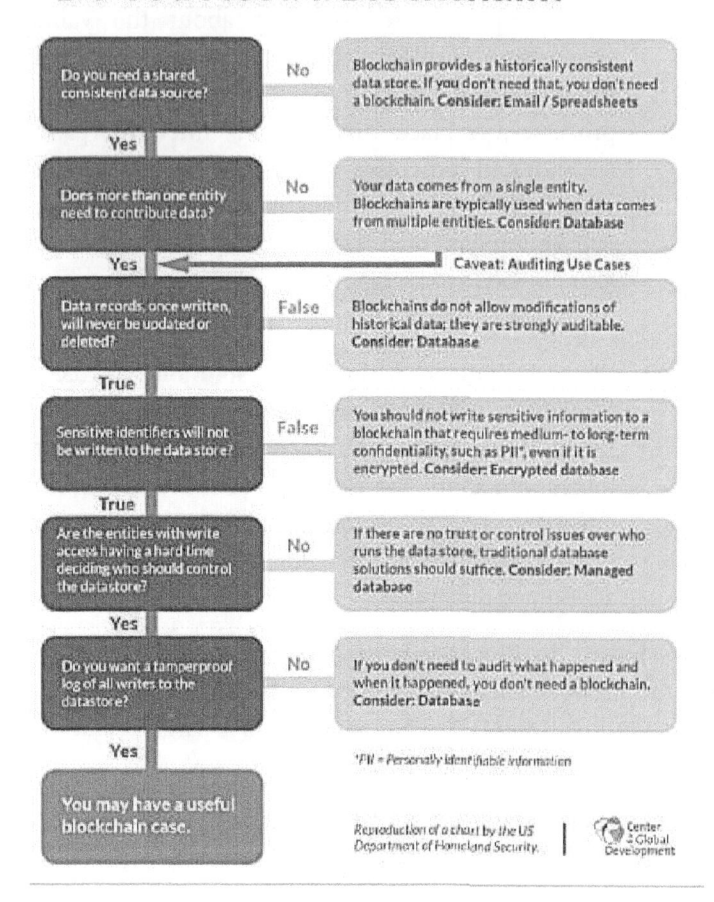

Question	Answer	Result
Do you need a shared, consistent data source?	No	Blockchain provides a historically consistent data store. If you don't need that, you don't need a blockchain. Consider: Email / Spreadsheets
Does more than one entity need to contribute data?	No	Your data comes from a single entity. Blockchains are typically used when data comes from multiple entities. Consider: Database (Caveat: Auditing Use Cases)
Data records, once written, will never be updated or deleted?	False	Blockchains do not allow modifications of historical data; they are strongly auditable. Consider: Database
Sensitive identifiers will not be written to the data store?	False	You should not write sensitive information to a blockchain that requires medium- to long-term confidentiality, such as PII*, even if it is encrypted. Consider: Encrypted database
Are the entities with write access having a hard time deciding who should control the datastore?	No	If there are no trust or control issues over who runs the data store, traditional database solutions should suffice. Consider: Managed database
Do you want a tamperproof log of all writes to the datastore?	No	If you don't need to audit what happened and when it happened, you don't need a blockchain. Consider: Database

If all answers lead to Yes/True: **You may have a useful blockchain case.**

*PII = Personally Identifiable Information

Reproduction of a chart by the US Department of Homeland Security. | Center for Global Development

Fig 4.2 Do you need Blockchain?

While the existing incumbents involved in running the businesses across the Governments are comfortable with the centralized approaches, the choice of a decentralized approach and Distributed Ledger Technology for the future is seen as a decision that may yield substantial returns, but are fraught with unforeseen risks. As the technology is still in its early stage of adoption, several factors need to be considered by the decision-makers to undertake the decision to migrate to the new paradigm. The following table gives a bird's eye view of the aspects to be considered for evaluating the suitability of a Distributed Ledger Technology-based solution.

Source:https://www.cgdev.org/publication/reassessing-expectations-Blockchain-and-development-cost-complexity

A high-powered committee with the involvement of the top management professionals should consider and analyze the various aspects of the problems to be tacked and evaluate the potential solutions.

4.4 Implementing Blockchain— The Six Sigma Perspective

A six-sigma-based approach with the following steps is the most appropriate way forward for a disruptive and new-generation technology like Blockchain.

The steps are outlined as follows:

1. **Define:** Identify and clearly outline the problem in hand to be solved.

2. **Measure:** Measure the key performance indicators that need to be impacted and evaluated for improvement and provide a measure for the Return on Investment. Benchmark with the best practices and other related/alternative solutions for assessing potential benefits.

3. **Analyze:** Analyze various options, potential solutions and available platforms to arrive at the best-case option by taking into account all possible parameters like investments required, resources and all implementation-related challenges.

4. **Design:** Architect the solution from various angles like data flows, entity relationships, information management, application development and technological and infrastructural considerations. Security considerations for the applications and all associated environments have to be thoroughly thought through and factored in.

The design has to thoroughly take into account various aspects like confidentiality, interoperability, confidentiality and privacy requirements, cybersecurity issues at various levels and the issues relating to compatibility with existing legacy systems and integration thereof.

As the existing centralized systems offer high transaction throughputs, the trade-off of the transaction volumes and speed with respect to the benefits like overall process-related gains, in the long run, need to be considered and factored in the design.

Seamless integration with the legacy systems, payment gateways and banking systems, ability to board new members, new processes and also drop them if required should be an important design element so that the assets and identities can conduct transactions across multiple platforms with ease through APIs or other appropriate middleware.

5. **Validate:** Undertake a two-stage approach of implementing a POC (Proof of Concept) for demonstrating the effectiveness of the solution without impacting the organizational systems, in case of an untested application without time-tested use case scenarios and then undertaking a pilot project by integrating the solutions in a limited and isolated environment.

Once all implementation-related issues are thoroughly evaluated, problems taken care and benefits validated, it is then time to scale up the solution to encompass a multi-department and multi-enterprise scenario.

Blockchain being a new technology paradigm, there is not much information available on the Return-on-Investments, though intuitively, most of the time it is very clear at the outset that the process excellence and the exponential benefits due to ecosystem collaboration are very much evident to the initiators with long-term vision.

When a Blockchain platform is created, all the applications possible between the participants on the same network can be envisioned and the returns quantified to evaluate the commercial viability with respect to the investments required.

From the service provider's point of view, Performance contracting that rewards the platform providers and the IT partners with a combination of fixed and savings-dependent variable revenue model can help get the Blockchain projects kicked off the ground in a win-win manner.

Different models for revenue generation like annual subscription, transaction-based pricing, maintenance and Smart Contract upgradation and maintenance can be considered with a possibility of increased usage not only from the existing applications but also due to the new business generation possibility with the increased network clientele aggregation possible.

4.5 The Consortium Approach to Implementing Blockchain

The growth of Consortia in the recent past in furthering the implementation and adoption of the Blockchain paradigm cannot be overstated.

How Networks & Business grow? A Blockchain ecosystem analogy to Contemperary Businesses

Degree of Centralisation		Private Permissioned	Partnership	Consortium	Hybrid (Permissioned + Public)	Public Permissioned	Public Permissionless
Features of Blockchain		Encryption	Immutability	Distribution	Decentralisation	Tokenisation	Disintermediation
Nodes/Ledger Accounts in relation to the stage and typr of Blockchain intervention	Number	1-2	3-7	8-15	16-1000	1001-5000	5001 & above
	Stage	PoC	Pilot	Production/Fair & fool proof governance	Expansion/Scaling, Increased Trust, Security, economies of scale, Analytics integration	Ecosystem Migration, Maximise benefits to the netwrok with pay per use approach	Global expansion, Interoperability across ecosystems max. benefits
	Phase	Explore	Engage	Process Reengineering	Supplement	Complement	Disrupt
Comparable cases							
Cloud		On Premise	VPN	Private Cloud	Hybrid	Proprietary Cloud	Public Cloud
Company Formation		Proprietary	Partnership	LLP	Private Ltd	Public Ltd	Public Listed
Network Connectivity		WiFi	Local Area Network	Wide Area Network	Wifi + Internet through Gateway	Internet with censors	Freely accessible Internet

The above order from left to right is not necessarily indicative across rows.

Fig 4.3 How do Networks and Businesses grow? A Blockchain ecosystem analogy and Contemporary Business.

Tradelens, a Blockchain consortium is a joint venture with IBM, the global leader in Blockchain solutions and infrastructure with an aim to make global trade more efficient, transparent and secure. Today, more than 60% of the global trade of containers is tracked through the TradeLens platform. Several ecosystem players comprising of transporters, ports, regulators, financial service companies, Warehouse providers, freight forwarders, etc., have now joined the network leading to substantial benefits to all concerned.

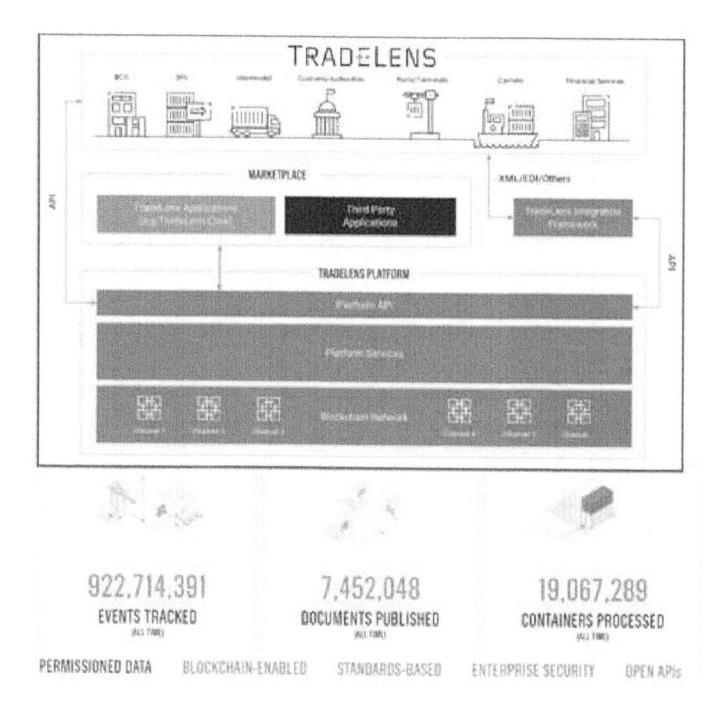

Fig 4.4 Tradelens architecture and impact https://docs.tradelens.com/learn/solution_architecture/

This has also led to the launch of 'Deliver' another large consortium led by Samsung Research labs, ABN Amro and Port of Rotterdam among others for a comprehensive ecosystem supporting platform in the same domain.

Several Blockchain consortia across various domains and industries are now growing from strength to strength. These consortia have matured Operational and governance mechanisms and are enabling industry-level movements at scale for adoption.

Consortia work on spurring the ecosystem for implementing Blockchain for common goals.

There are consortia that are built around Technology platforms like Hyperledger, R3, Ethereum, etc., which are focused on leveraging the specific properties of the platforms.

There are consortia that are created for vertical integration of ecosystems like Supply Chain, document lifecycle management and are initiated by a dominant player or a Government to port more and more of the customers and vendors on to the platform.

There are also consortia which are facilitated by regulators for offering Government services to result in transparent, corruption-free services to the citizens that can also check potential frauds. Blockchain applications for land records of various Governments across the world, Income Tax information sharing with banks and financial institutions by the Income Tax department, Cellular operator network to regulate unauthorized commercial communication by TRAI (Telecom Regulatory Authority of India) in collaboration with leading Technology, platform and infrastructure companies are a few such examples.

However, as the consortium grows in size, various players who are peers in the industry who are hitherto competitors, come together and join the consortium to jointly leverage economies of scale and also solve common problems they face, like frauds, cybersecurity threats, regulatory compliances, industry bargaining power with consolidation and end-to-end traceability.

Thus, the consortium grows both horizontally and vertically to encompass the entire business domain in its entirety.

But for this, the governance of the consortium must be of the highest standards to earn the confidence of all the participants, a very difficult act given the complexity of interactions and competing priorities. Most often, the business identity of the consortium should be distinct and keep above-the-board interactions with the individual entities. It should be led as a separate company or a society with its own competent governing council and a viable and sustainable business model.

Various issues like the equitable sharing of investments, profits and contributions, the value of intellectual property created should be governed with utmost balance and integrity. The fear that the dominant players could undermine the confidentiality and privacy of the data governed by the Blockchain should be addressed to enable trust within the consortium members and give rise to the decentralized governance in both letter and spirit.

Some of the notable consortia in operation are described in the following:

Food Trust – Promoted by IBM and Walmart.

In 2017, a group of ten Fortune 500 food processing and trading organizations, Walmart, Dole, Nestle, Tyson, GSF, Unilever, McCormick, Kroger, Driscoll's and McLane joined hands with IBM to launch Food Trust, a global Blockchain consortium for increasing traceability of food items across their supply chains.

The consortium enlists producers, suppliers, manufacturers, retailers, processors, regulators and consumers from across the food and grocery industry for a safer food supply chain with real-time automation, tracking, traceability and ability to pinpoint consignments in case of rotten/expired products, through a simple QR scan. The network tracks and monitors in real-time, complete information on the origin, transport and storage conditions, ownership and location movements over a Hyperledger Fabric-inspired Blockchain platform.

OOC—Oil and Blockchain consortium—is promoted by seven founding member companies: Chevron, ConocoPhillips, Equinor, ExxonMobil, Hess, Pioneer Natural Resources and Repsol and governed by a Board comprised of representatives from these companies. OOC has partnered with Data Gumbo, a Blockchain-as-a-Service (BaaS) company that has created a massively interconnected Blockchain network GumboNet™ for industrial companies including oil and gas.

The consortium aims to develop applications focused on the Oil and Gas industry by improving the process of reconciliation and eliminating disputes by increasing transparency, provide a single source of truth for shared data, increase security, reducing costs and improving the timeliness of contract executions. They are also working on standardization of data, processes, improving compliance and driving standard-setting through the industry alignment on key Blockchain components like cryptography, Smart Contract, consensus and governance aspects.

Boeing, the aviation major joined hands with Honeywell automation and other ecosystem partners of the aviation supply chain to launch Go Direct trade for tracking the provenance and safety adherence standards of aerospace spare parts.

In India, the Income Tax department is working with IT major Infosys on a Blockchain consortium with leading banks to provide a single source of truth for income tax filings of the citizens under various sections, to prevent frauds related to the same in availing loans and claiming excess deductions. The Income Tax department is playing the role of the ecosystem facilitator while also bringing the angle of the regulator. The consortium aims to explore multiple use cases for a wider adoption involving all the citizens and the players in the entire financial system.

Telecom Regulator of India TRAI joined hands with IT major Tech Mahindra and other leading companies like IBM and Microsoft to implement a Distributed ledger application on the Hyperledger Fabric platform to check Unauthorized Commercial Communication (UCC).

Likewise, there are many more consortia operating in the financial domain like WeTrade, Voltron, Marcopolo, HKTFP, etc., focusing on trade finance applications.

Sl No	Name of Consortium	Domain	Type of consortium	Platform
	Together We Win - The Blockchain Consortia on the move across the world			
1	Hyperledger	Enterprise & Government	Technology focused	Group of projects
2	Enterprise Ethereum Alliance	Enterprise & Government	Technology focused	Group of projects
3	R3	Enterprise & Government	Technology focused	Corda
4	IBM Food Trust	FMCG	Business Focused	Hyperledger Fabric
5	IBM Tradelens	Global Logistics	Business Focused	Hyperledger Fabric
6	IBM TravelPort	Travel & Leisure	Business Focused	Hyperledger Fabric
7	Deliver	Global Logistics	Business Focused	R3 + HyFabric
8	OOC	Oil & Gas	Business Focused	GumboNet
9	Global Shipping Business Network	Global Logistics	Business Focused	Hyperledger Fabric
10	Trusted IOT Alliance	Smart city, M2X	Tech & Business	Hyperledger Fabric
11	Mediledger	Healthcare, Pharma	Business Focused	Mediledger
12	MarcoPolo	Trade Finance	Business Focused	R3 Corda
13	We.Trade	Trade Finance	Business Focused	Hyperledger Fabric
14	Hashed Health	Pharma	Business Focused	Hyperledger Fabric
15	Voltron	Trade Finance	Business Focused	R3 Corda
16	BATAVIA	Tarade Finance	Business Focused	Hyperledger Fabric
17	MOBI	Transport & Environment	Business Focused	IOTA/ HyFabric
18	Energy Web Foundation	Clean Energy	Business Focused	Energy WebChain
19	Chinese Business Alliance	Finance & Commodities	Business Focused	China Ledger
20	B3I	Insurance	Business Focused	R3 Corda
21	Japan Exchange Group	Finance & Commodities	Business Focused	Multiple
22	Financial Blockchain Shenzhen Consortium (FISCO)	Finance	Business Focused	Ethereum
23	IBM Health Utility Network	Health care	Business Focused	Hyperledger Fabric
24	GTCN (Global Trade Connectivity Network)	Trade Finance	Business Focused	HKTFP(Hongkong Trade & Finance Problem)
25	Komgo	Trade Finance	Business Focused	Ethereum
26	GoTrade	Auto Supplychain	Business Focused	Hyperledger Fabric
27	ITD	Finance	Business Focused	Hyperledger Fabric
28	India Trade Connect	Trade Finance	Business Focused	R3 Corda

Fig 4.5 Together We win—The Blockchain Consortia on the move across the world.

It can be seen from the above various applications that for a successful Blockchain implementation, the following factors act as catalysts and facilitators:

1. Problem: A compelling problem to solve

2. Promoting/founding group: A key ecosystem player preferable a dominant player in the industry,

3. Technology partner: A competent technology partner to facilitate implementation.

4. Process gaps: High possibility of Business process reengineering to streamline inter-organizational processes and implement systematic interactions.

5. Infrastructure partner: A technology infrastructure partner can expand the technical bandwidth and facilitate large-scale implementations at scale and

6. Blockchain platform: A sound and tested Blockchain platform amenable for enterprise applications like Hyperledger Fabric, R3 Corda, Quorum, Sawtooth, etc.

More on companies, consortia, countries catalyzing the Blockchain ecosystem, challenges in Blockchain implementation and the profile of the team members required to implement the solutions are discussed in the subsequent sessions.

4.6 Are you Ready to Start the Blockchain Project?

So you want to start a Blockchain?

This is what most of the businesses today are grappling with and are looking for ways and means to start applying Blockchain in their business.

There are a few ways in which you can get into Blockchain.

I. Leverage any of the Public Blockchain platforms and use it as 'Trust as a Service' You can use the

Public Blockchain-based DAPPS to notarize your documents and create a proof of existence for your personal document, IPs, wills, agreements and the like so that the Time-stamp and the Blockchain record can prove the existence of the document.

II. Create a private Blockchain network for your small group of company employees or a group of your business partners by using open-source platforms like Private Ethereum, Hyperledger Fabric, R3 Corda, etc. There are many more choices but these are the popular ones. This involves setting up one or two mining/orders/notary nodes with replication for DR to act as the Trusted Third Party that creates a foolproof transaction record and then model long the transactions.

Once the mining and consensus noted are identified by the administrator, it is time to identify and provide certificates for the other members to join the network along with corresponding access rights. The network can be expanded as more member nodes join and decentralized applications also referred to as chain codes or smart contracts are created to model the business rules that reflect the transactions that update the ledger state on the Blockchain. Large MNCs like HSBC with branches across the world and Governments have found this model useful. This approach is also a starting point for several current consortium projects like TradeLens and Food Trust.

III. In the next stage, the network can grow larger into a consortium with sound governance and administration if everything goes well in due course.

IV. Another option is to create a Quorum of highly credible organizations manning nodes as the Consensus network with resource-efficient algorithms like POA, DPOS, RBFT, etc. With this in place, there is the possibility of launching a Public Permissioned network supporting a larger ecosystem with several decentralized applications in place.

A public Permissionless Blockchain follows the next step but this space is already taken by Blockchain like Bitcoin and Ethereum which are running the risk of falling on the wrong side of environment sustainability.

It is important to note that as stated earlier, the POC phase, without integrating the application into the legacy systems of the clients is meant to demonstrate the utility of Blockchain for effectively solving the problems outlined and in dramatically improving upon the performance parameters. This phase also demonstrates the potential ROI that can be expected out of the investments and what would entail the same. The pilot phase is undertaken by integrating the application into a small localized environment to ensure that the disruption to the existing operations if any is minimized and repercussions fully understood. This also validates the learnings from the POC phase and sets up the tone for a wider intra and inter-enterprise adoption. Production and Scale-up phases are now ready to take off with all the bottlenecks including the technology glitches and starting trouble from people involved taken care of. As the operations grow into the Consortium phase (or a collection of departments), the importance of governance mechanisms has to be well understood as this can make or break the entire arrangement leading to the collapse of multi-enterprise systems. Governing consortia is a tight-rope walking business and needs to be undertaken with the utmost sensitivity as outlined in the 'Challenges' section.

Networks have "network effects." Adding a new participant increases the value of the network for all existing participants: **Naval** Ravikant (one of the most influential Blockchain evangelists in the world).

Case Study – Blockchain adoption by a global leader

In March 2020, global automobile major Toyota Motor Corporation decided to explore and exploit the disruptive potential of Blockchain technology. After carefully evaluating the various benefits and potential value accretion on account of BCT, Toyota Blockchain Lab was incorporated to research opportunities and use cases, conduct POCs and pilots and grow the practice by roping in its partners across the value chain.

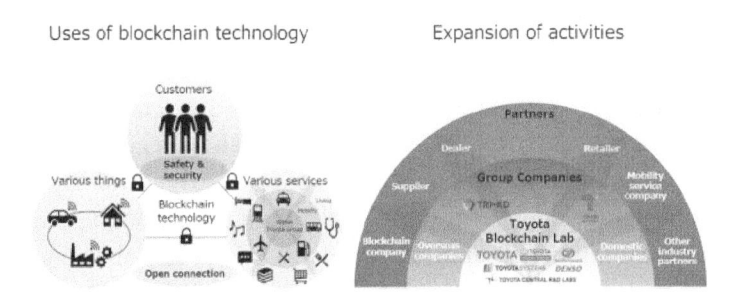

Fig: 4.6 Toyota Motor company's Blockchain action plan. Source: https://global.toyota/en/newsroom/corporate/31827481.html

The lab plans to collaborate with technology companies and other ecosystem players to form a consortium. This example depicts a typical way large organizations strategize and execute their Blockchain projects in the long run.

Case Study: Blockchain application to empower Start-ups.

(Courtesy: www.smartchainers.com, Chennai)

Setting up and growing a Startup is one of the most challenging tasks. The percentage of successful Start-ups that make it from the ideas stage to a large organization or achieve a successful and sustainable equity infusion is very miniscule.

However, the Start-ups have to undergo the rigmarole of setting up Pvt. Ltd. Companies in case they want to be seen as serious players by potential customers.

Meanwhile, there are many compliance issues to be tacked. Even after that, in most cases of private limited companies, we see that they are not only short on compliance-adherence, but are also at a loss of words when potential investors discuss the valuations and promoters' shares due to laxity in adhering to accounting practices to value their efforts that led to the valuation in the first place.

Blockchain with its ability to offer transparent, immutable, tamper-evident data and also regulatory oversight to Government authorities and Registrar of Companies poses a great solution to manage real-time shareholding patterns and valuations of companies, especially the LLP and small-time Pvt. Ltd. organizations that cannot afford the accounting practices of the big.

- Delaware allows corporations to maintain shareholder lists and other business records stored on a Blockchain.
- California is considering a bill that would formally recognize Blockchain signatures and other data as electronic records.
- Blockchain Records will now be accepted as Legal evidence—China's Super Court.

168 ♦ *Blockchain for Non IT Professionals*

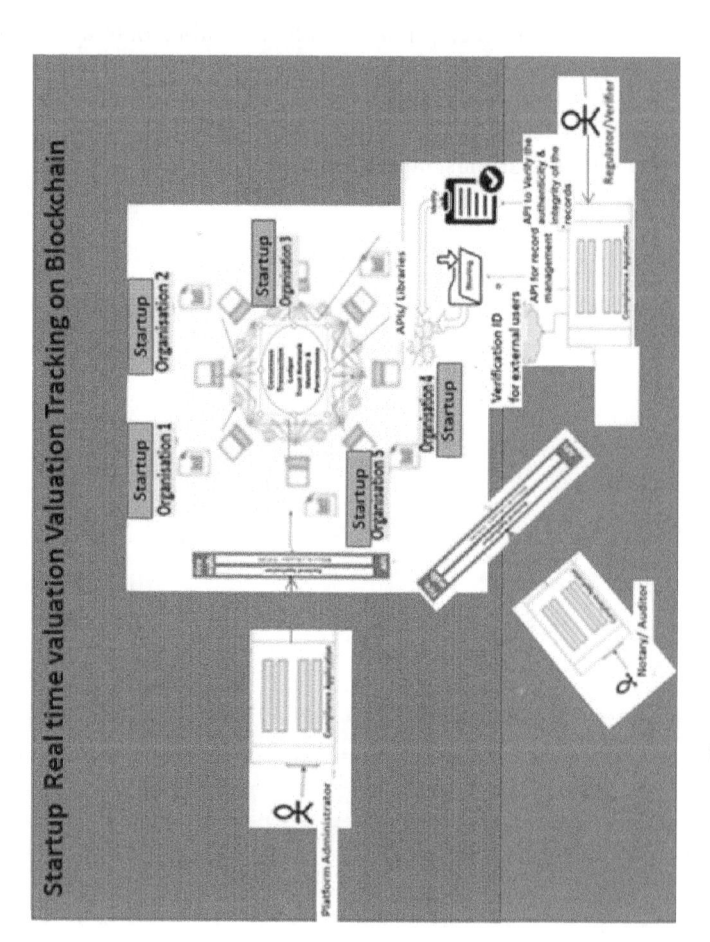

Fig 4.7 Startup Real-Time Valuation Tracking on Blockchain.

The system allows administrators to leverage the help of auditors and immutable, real-time and transparent Blockchain records to provide a real-time valuation track to all entrepreneurs in their Blockchain wallets that could also be endorsed by lawmakers and accepted by potential investors.

Fig 4.8 Blockchain Certified LLPs.

Blockchain can enable organizations to demonstrate regulatory compliance while eliminating long processes and documentation that often accompanies these processes.

The system administrator and the auditors will work with the Startup founders in sticking to the shareholder agreements, recording every milestone and value additions with their digital signatures to reflect the same in the respective shareholdings on a real-time basis in their Blockchain wallets.

At any point, a complete record of the shareholding and valuation track for any start up on the Blockchain can be printed with Blockchain acting like the Trusted Third Party with a provision for regulatory oversight.

It is important that the Blockchain's administration and Consensus are managed by a highly trusted group of organizations/professionals with an above-the-board track record.

Case Study: Blockchain application to combat Corona Virus Spread (nCovid19)

(Courtesy—Astra Quark Digi-Solutions, Chennai).

nCovid19 is a type of Corona Virus that spread like a contagion across the world in early 2020 causing the death of thousands of citizens. Astra Quark Digi-Solutions, a Blockchain Startup in Chennai envisaged the launch of a Blockchain consortium and a solution under the name 'Curehona' to address the spread of the virus in a multipronged manner. Some of the key advantages such a platform can offer to combat the deadly diseases are envisaged as follows:

- Verifiable, Immutable patient, treatment, protocol, progress and other records.
- Need-based expert intervention wherever required.
- AI and Analytics-based insights on the efficacy of various treatments/medicines/protocols/healthcare service providers etc.

AQDL identified the following value additions that a Blockchain-based approach can provide to combat any health care emergency situation like the nCovid19 pandemic.

Value propositions of Blockchain for Corona Virus (nCovid19) control

- Track-and-Trace the Corona-affected persons
- Monitor day-to-day health conditions
- Comprehensive treatment management especially using approved allopathic and alternative medicines
- Connect patients to health workers doctors/facilities
- Treatment protocol management
- Patient cure and improvement monitoring and management
- Alternative medicines efficacy management
- Record/upload authentic experiences of patients and share the link to the video on a public distributed ledger
- Supply chain management—Provenance and availability of genuine medicines against prescriptions, Product and Vaccine verification
- Facilitate Charitable activities and track donation life cycle
- Insurance Processing and claims reconciliation

The company set itself on its task to mobilize a global coordinated effort toward its efforts to champion this technology-enabled platform with the following objectives.

1. Multinational health firms can participate in a Blockchain-based platform that will connect local hospitals and health institutions in potential zones into which the virus may spread.

2. Local hospitals can record medical data about patients who show flu or virus-like symptoms in the form of a public ID (patients will remain non-identifiable).

3. This data can be tracked by the health firms in order to predict the spread of the virus based on the state of patients' medical statistics.

4. Countries will be able to strengthen their preventive measures in the areas where the virus can potentially spread—e.g., increasing the workforce of medical staff, providing medical supplies.

5. The platform can offer an opportunity for all stakeholders and patients to exchange information, support and services in a trusted environment with regulatory oversight.

6. Provide an opportunity for innovators to record ideas with provenance and establish proof of idea ownership

Hash Log (https://hashlog.io/) offers a Blockchain-enabled portal (powered by the platform Hedera Hashgraph) for real-time data collation and visualization to enable the netizens across the world to update themselves about the various statistics connected with this deadly disease, thus alerting the Governments and people across the world to understand the trends and the seriousness of the pandemic enabling them to be on guard.

Blockchain technology is surely having an immense utility to combat global problems by rebuilding the broken trust in global supply chains, demand, supply and financing mechanisms, information sharing and enabling a coordinated and trusted research across the world.

In fact, all the global leading countries should work together and form a new-age United Nations-supported Blockchain platform that acts as a 'Trust bridge' for a collective and collaborative approach to solve the global problems that are proving to be far more dangerous than the World Wars as we know!

In April 2020, World Health Organization (WHO) in collaboration with world's leading firms like IBM and Microsoft launched MiPasa (www.mipasa.org) **MiPasa Blockchain platform** to combat Coronavirus by connecting a multidisciplinary super-group of health professionals, privacy experts, and software developers, backed by leading technology companies and commercial entities.

Utilizing powerful analytics and privacy tools, MiPasa works to gather reliable, quality data, and make it easily accessible to the appropriate entities in order to efficiently battle the ongoing Coronavirus pandemic in a humane, fair and more sustainable manner.

Government of India planned to implement the following Blockchain solutions to effectively manage the health hazards like nCovid19 Pandemics.

1. Blockchain-based medical record management for all the patients to seamlessly and securely connect their medical records across all providers by retaining the patient's privacy.

2. Blockchain-based information-sharing mechanism to all the participants in the medical system like hospitals, regulators, service providers, patients, diagnostic centers and care providers to share authentic and trusted information required for a holistic patient-care and treatment, including spare capacities, critical care medical equipment, ambulance services, etc.

3. Blockchain-based transportation management system to seamlessly integrate with vehicle registration, driving license and commercial tax collection systems to allow a smooth traffic flow across the national highways for speedy transfer of essentials and health care goods.

Case Study: A model Consortium—IBM Walmart Food Trust for Supply chain traceability and efficiency.

According to the World Health Organization, food poisoning affects 10% of the population causing over four hundred thousand deaths every year. Food fraud resulting from the substitution of actual food contained in packages with cheaper substitutes and also fake products causes a loss of over 40 Billion US Dollars to manufacturers worldwide as per PWC.

The damage caused to the delay in tracing the source of contamination in case of improper transportation conditions and damaged goods is immeasurable and leads to loss of public trust in the supply chain and also loss of face and business for all the actors in the supply chain viz., farmers, manufacturers, wholesalers, retailers, restaurants, etc.

E.coli breakout in 2006 wiped out the entire spinach industry due to the delay in tracking down the source of contamination. Pork mislabeling scandal in 2011 in China, fox meat contamination in donkey meat boxes in China, and horse meat contamination in lamb meat in European Union have resulted in the breakdown of supply chains in the respective regions.

Faced with increasing problems of trust erosion and food contamination, global leader Walmart joined hands with IBM and built a Permissioned Blockchain platform to reduce the tracking time of food products like Mango and Pork from several weeks to a few seconds. Today, the association has grown into a large consortium with thousands of participants across the globe deriving the benefits of food traceability, accurate estimation of shelf life of products in the supply chain, assurance of proper transportation for freshness, eliminate food fraud and fake product substitution, estimate demand and manufacture accordingly to eliminate expired goods and waste in the system and above all gain the trust of their consumers and business partners.

Food Trust is a classic example of a Private Permissioned Blockchain growing into a vibrant Public Permissioned Consortium Blockchain platform thus growing across the stages mentioned in the earlier section.

If you don't 'Run' your Consortium well, You will be 'Ruined' spectacularly, thanks to the 'I.'

It is the collective approach and keeping the 'I' or selfish, centralized approach at bay that wins in the long term.

The study of Food Trust Consortium offers several lessons outlined below, that can help in successfully creating, developing, maintaining and growing Blockchain consortium.

1. A compelling value proposition that is driven by a great purpose and also reflects a lot of business sense, offering immense value to all the participants that can be offered by using the Blockchain technology is a basic prerequisite to set up, populate and propagate a consortium.

2. A clear outline of the potential benefits and communication of 'WIIFM' (What is in it for me) to each and every type of participant in the targeted ecosystem is a must. The consortium participants should draw up a set of shared common goals that can be addressed by the system and should use this to create the 'Vision, Mission, Values and Goals' for the collaborative effort.

3. Convenient on-boarding methodology and instruction manuals that explain in a concise and clear manner about the process to adapt, operate and participate in the system will go a long way. This will help in quickly appealing to a larger participant base and getting them on board to improve the viability of the platform through the network effect.

4. A strong and tested Technology platform with a sound leadership group that can inspire confidence for a 'Permanent' set up is a must for the consortium to scale seamlessly.

5. A long-term approach based on solid foundations will result in sustainable growth. While the initial

few use cases should indeed be compelling for the consortium to take off, a systematic approach starting with use case identification and prioritization, focused POC execution executed with success and a demonstrable value leading to an actionable pilot is a must if you want to succeed in the long run.

6. A consortium promoted by a dominant player in the industry, capable of exercising influence over a large network of potential industry participants will go a long way in helping up the Consortia taking off from the ground in a quick time.

7. Governance is the 'glue' that can hold the consortium together and it must address the various entity-specific issues like data privacy, IPs and entity-specific requirements in a fair and transparent manner with any of the founding partners acting in a high-handed manner to take advantage of their position. Any such attempt by the founding members or dominant parties will sound a death knell to the Consortium's growth.

Thus, several specific technological, business and governance issues have to be taken into account for a balanced approach for the success of the Consortium in the long run.

Several Blockchain consortia and decentralized applications like Origin Trial are now operating leading to a wholesale migration of the Pharma and Food Product supply chains into the new era of trust and transparency for the consumers worldwide. It is only a matter of time when you can scan a QR code on an imported product's package in the duty-free shop in the airport and satisfy yourself about its genuineness or reject a product from a chemist, however much trusted or big he is, because the medicine he is selling could not provide the QR code for scanning to provide the Blockchain-enabled traceability to the manufacturer and hence could risk being considered a fake drug!

Blockchain potentials for offering solutions to the day-to-day problems faced by most of the corporates are sought to be addressed by an Augmented Distributed Ledger Technology platform acting as a Trusted Third Party with the Triple entry-accounting concept that has been extensively discussed in this book has been researched immensely by several new-age Blockchain-inspired organizations. Aurigraph, a new-age DLT company has been generous to offer some of their unique solutions to the readers of this book so that the potential of this technology can be well appreciated beyond doubt. The same has been explained in the following (Courtesy: Subbu Jois, subbu@aurigraph.io). Some of the problems that can be solved using the Distributed Ledger Technology and the corresponding solutions that the technology offers are explained below.

DLT for Telecom Interconnect Reconciliation

PROBLEM: Mobile Telecom service providers need to settle Interconnect fees for calls originating and landing across networks, which is further complicated when there are third party tower companies and International long-distance calling and roaming services.

Interconnect charges are applicable for:

- Mobile-to-mobile connectivity employs "netting" over a period for settlement, which can result in the following issues:
    - Data downloads across multiple tower companies imply multiple settlements to be

handled by the service provider, especially when customers are mobile

- Roaming and International Long-Distance calls have extended netting and settlement cycles which are further aggravated due to dynamic pricing practices and volatile currency exchange rates.

DLT Solution

Aurigraph DLT can offer a real-time reconciliation solution across multiple mobile service providers in an open Clearing House architecture using Triple entry-accounting principles. Aurigraph Enterprise Nodes integrated with the CDR systems of the mobile service provider may be reconciled with the corresponding mobile service provider using Aurigraph interconnect DApps. Each service provider will be able to reconcile and settle all the CDRs the same day with little or no manual intervention

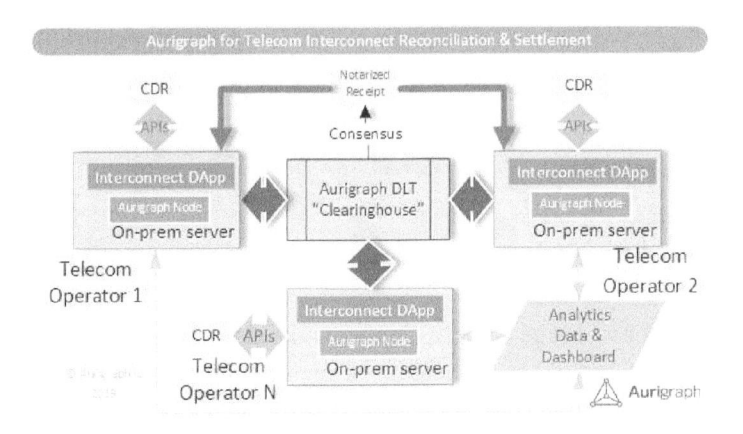

Fig 4.9 Aurigraph for Telecom Interconnect Reconciliation and Settlement.

Benefits

- Reconcile and Settle millions of CDRs in real-time between multiple mobile operators at a fraction of the cost

- Predictable cashflow

- Complete data security as all reconciliation and settlement is electronically executed without any human intervention

Multiparty Track-and-Trace-Solution Using DLT

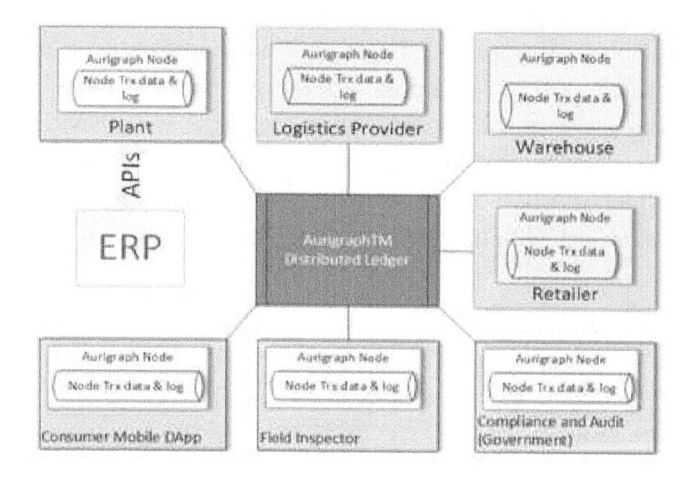

Fig 4.10 Aurigraph Track-and Trade solution.

PROBLEM: Large Supply Chains and value chains require the tracking of the movement of material and transactions across multiple stakeholders. The absence of transaction and material traceability is a logistically expensive and tedious process, requiring expensive and time-consuming inventory audits. In recall scenarios, the time taken to trace and retrieve each and every unit of the product takes six months to three years, which can result in severe damage to the business, reputation and profits.

DLT Solution

DLT offers a solution for Track-and-Trace to offer inter-integration across multiple software and platforms to track all items in a value chain from its origin to the final consumer be it by the vendor, batch, and date of manufacture, plant and place of origin. The solution will require Aurigraph Enterprise Node to be integrated with ERP/CRM and similar back-end systems of each stakeholder in the value chain to capture the progression of the transaction and product until its final owner. The public ledger will provide a unified dashboard to help Track-and-Trace.

Benefits

Aurigraph's DLT Track-and-Trace solution can help in tracing a unit of the item to the last recorded possession in a matter of minutes, and bring down tracking and tracing costs by over 90%, thereby reducing the risk of statutory penalties and

- Reduce effort, time and cost to trace and retrieve products recalled
- Reduce legal costs and damages

Real-time Financial Reconciliations

PROBLEM: Financial systems and transactions generate a great number of suspense accounts. A Suspense Account is a general ledger account in which amounts are temporarily recorded. The Suspense Account is used because the appropriate general ledger account could not be determined at the time that the transaction was recorded. In Fintech applications, every transaction goes through a series of suspense accounts before being committed to the final ledger and the general ledger. However, addition, posting and trial balance errors may be generated in the process needing compensating errors resulting in further entropy with about 1% error rate. The cost of correcting the errors and exceptions form a significant amount of enterprises' operational expenses.

DLT Solution

Aurigraph offers direct reconciliation between two ledgers without the need to introduce suspense accounts for temporarily "holding" a transaction. Transactions can get posted to the corresponding ledger through Aurigraph Enterprise Nodes integrating with each ledger to eliminate reconciliation due to false-negative transactions, leading to the exception. The transactions would be held in the respective Aurigraph Enterprise Node till being posted to the ledger, thereby eliminating the need for suspense accounts and their incumbent errors and exceptions.

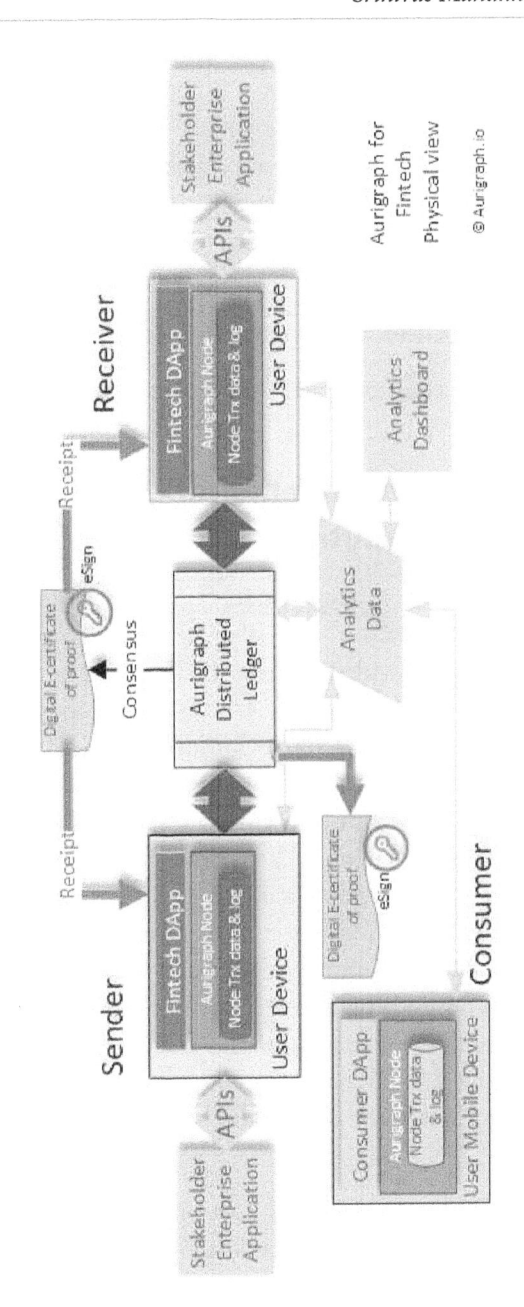

Fig 4.11 Simplifying Financial Reconciliation using DLT.

Benefits

- Eliminating false-negative errors and exceptions while capturing human errors, eliminating the need for manual intervention to manage such exception, thereby bringing down operational expenses by over 50%

- Improving customer experience and satisfaction

- Improving cashflow and profits correspondingly

4.7 Challenges in Implementing Blockchain Solutions

We have seen many exciting features and benefits of Blockchain implementation and also several successful use cases spanning individual entities (HSBC inter-branch remittances of over 250 billion US Dollars), to intra network applications (JPM Coin), Consortia (Food Trust, Trade lens, Deliver), decentralized applications (Origin Trial) and Bitcoin itself and also Governments embracing Blockchain like Estonia, Dubai, UK, Sweden, Switzerland, Belgium and the like. Bitcoin and Ethereum continue to be successful live applications for a long time and seem to be evolving against multiple attacks and shortcomings through various improvement programs from time to time. However, the number of successful and thriving use cases in the Permissioned Blockchain space is still a handful and experiments continue to be done and ecosystems continue to evolve.

The following figure describes some of the challenges faced in implementing Blockchain solutions.

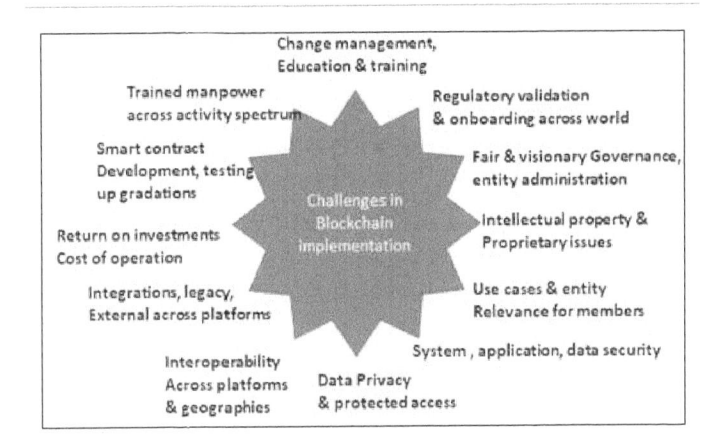

```
                Change management,
                Education & training
   Trained manpower
   across activity spectrum        Regulatory validation
                                   & onboarding across world
   Smart contract
   Development, testing            Fair & visionary Governance,
   up gradations                   entity administration
                   Challenges in
                   Blockchain      Intellectual property &
   Return on investments   implementation   Proprietary issues
   Cost of operation

   Integrations, legacy,           Use cases & entity
   External across platforms       Relevance for members

                            System, application, data security
       Interoperability
       Across platforms    Data Privacy
       & geographies       & protected access
```

Fig: 4.12 Challenges faced while implementing Blockchain solutions.

The Central Bank Digital Currency on a DLT is the most important enabling factor that can accelerate this transition to a decentralized world for trusted transactions across machines and humans.

Unlike centralized systems that require the respective entities to make decisions regarding their investments, Blockchain implementation requires a paradigm shift and involves the communication of a very different nature between different enterprises or competing units. This gives rise to many challenges and some of the key ones are mentioned below:

  I. **Performance management:** Database systems for Blockchain systems are still primitive and given the permanent/immutable nature of the data and the need for storing Smart Contracts it is implied that the performance of the Blockchain systems cannot match the traditional centralized systems.

Hence utmost care has to be taken to decide on the applicability of Blockchain solution and the modeling of data storage and program execution on-chain and off-chain for optimal trade-offs. The usage of APIs to integrate the Blockchain data with the external data in the organizations or with other external applications and data sources for an integrated view and the overall picture needs to be well understood and implemented.

II. **Versioning and Upgradation**: Since Blockchain is a new-generation and fast-evolving technology, there needs to be continuous upgradation of the software versions and implementation of patches for upgradation. This is a challenge when you have to update past records especially in view of the immutability. This needs to be factored in while designing the solution. Solutions should be architected by keeping in mind the immutability-aspect of the ledger-posted transaction records and the difficulty thereof to update the same later.

III. **Appeal for a larger target market:** The network effort is a very important aspect of Blockchain and the bigger the network, the better is the viability. Hence the decision to implement a Blockchain-based solution should keep the big picture in mind about the potential compelling appeal to a large target partner base and the staying power of the initiators for a long term till the traction scales for sustainability.

IV. **Protecting Copyrights, confidential information and IPs:** Privacy and confidentiality of company-specific information is a must when competitors are collaborating on a platform as a dent to this can affect the survival of the organization. Hence this is a critical factor that needs to be seriously addressed in enterprise applications.

Personal identifiable information is stored on mutable off-chain records with adequate privacy measures to protect the rights of the participants as per the data protection regulations.

V. **Complexity in building networks:** As more and more people are discovering the utility of implementing Blockchain solutions, several consortia and individual organizational efforts are surfacing. Since Blockchain is essentially an inter-enterprise platform, the importance of being a part of a larger network to derive its full benefit cannot be understated.

The cost and effort of building networks are daunting and the initiators and founders of the networks need a lot of patience, staying power and long-term vision. Also, it is important to consider the option of joining existing networks with an open mind. The participants should have a paradigm shift in thinking from an individualistic approach to a collective approach to solving problems to work in an ecosystem in a win-win manner.

VI. **Managing the middlemen from the old school:** Blockchain platform abstracts several services hitherto provided by Trusted Third Parties acting as middlemen. There will be a lot of resistance from the old order and displaced middlemen to create hurdles for adoption and stymie the process. The elimination of middlemen should not result in inconvenience to the transacting peers and the value provided by the platform should be much more than the cost incurred by the peers. Being a new technology, the ease of access, operation and user experience should be ensured for seamless and smooth transitions

VII. **Secured storage of Private Keys.:** Blockchain uses PKI based Identity Management systems and cryptographic algorithms extensively.

All the transaction participants are identified with their public keys and digitally sign their transactions with their private keys for security, privacy, confidentiality and non-repudiation. Hence it is imperative that the keys are handled with utmost security with appropriate revocation and replacement mechanisms in place for keys of disengaged/suspended members, key losers and for those whose keys have been compromised.

4.8 Roles and Responsibilities for a Blockchain Organization

The top two skillsets for Blockchain entrepreneurs, in order: Technology development, Community development: **Naval Ravikant**

Blockchain is only 25% Technology and 75% Communication, Collaboration and Management and one needs to take into account 'Why, What, Who, Where' and 'How to bring all this together' to make a business sense and viability for a sustainable operation. Though in the long run, things could fall in place, in the short run, many challenges need to be overcome including inertia and resistance for change from incumbent practices. A passion for change and technology-sense to see the big picture of Digital

Transformation as a combination of all emerging technologies including Cloud, IOT, Big Data, AI&ML-powered analytics, etc.is very much desirable in Blockchain practitioners.

Hence a variety of skilled professionals are required starting from developers, analysts, architects, network administrators, security and testing professionals, Cloud service managers, administrators, consultants, middleware, API developers, system integrator, business managers and client partners.

Correspondingly, there is scope for different types of professionals with a good understanding of decentralized and distributed systems and also passionate about this technology paradigm, as follows.

Blockchain Practice lead/Strategic Consultant: The consultants should also have experience in corporate strategy and a good idea of Blockchain applications with respect to Enterprise transformation concepts like Enterprise Architecture, Six Sigma, Business Process reengineering and other emerging technologies.

The Practice head should be adept at communicating the case for Blockchain effectively through examples, analogies and user stories for various use cases in conjunction with all emerging technologies.

Functional Consultants: Sector-specific domain experts and the ability for strategic thinking with an understanding of business processes in the respective domain apart from a very good understanding of all the concepts of DLT. They should be able to garner and convince the ecosystem players to partner for creating a network together for implementing Blockchain solutions.

Consortium Management: There are over 30 leading Blockchain consortia across the world. This is a growing phenomenon and in the future, almost every business will be a member of some consortium or the other. The consortia will generate huge employment across various activities required for consortium management, marketing, development and Governance. This requires the abilities like communication skills, teamwork, business development, administration and financial management to deliver a win-win proposition.

Integration specialists: Integration specialists are the key to implementing Blockchain solutions due to the inter-enterprise nature of the platform and also due to extensive use of Rest services, SDK, API, IOT, multiple clouds, Analytics and Big Data platforms and the need for interoperability.

Identity Management: Permissioned Blockchains offer accountability, traceability, cybersecurity and risk management. There is a need to adhere to privacy regulations. Blockchain finds extensive applications in KYC and uniquely identifying beneficiaries to eliminate fakes and also screen transaction partners for foolproof access control, authentication and authorization. Interoperability across traditional and Blockchain platforms, across the Blockchain platform in multiple geographies, entails seamless and secured Identity Management which requires high-level expertise in Identity platforms, methodologies, solutions and concepts.

Blockchain application developers: Blockchain application developers are programmers who create applications and Smart Contracts in languages like C++, Python, Node JS, Java, Solidity, G Lang, etc. that users interact with and are hosted on the Blockchain.

Blockchain Solution Architect: The Blockchain Solution Architect is responsible for designing, assigning and connecting Blockchain solution components and interacts with developers, network administrators, UX designers, and IT Operations to develop end-to-end technical documentation for Blockchain solutions. Should have a deep understanding of Digital Transformation, DEVOPS, API development process, Enterprise Architecture, Six Sigma and Business Process reengineering with exposure to Linux, CLI, Cloud, Docker, GIT, API, etc.

Business Analyst: Business Analyst does a detailed research of the clients' requirements, undertakes research of relevant use cases, potential use cases and creates detailed documentation of Business requirements through storyboarding, writing requirement specifications and analysis of the requirements, solution specification, to enable formulation of an appropriate solution.

Blockchain Project Manager: Blockchain project/program manager can create, manage and monitor detailed project plans for various use cases across the POC, Pilot to Scale-up stages. Has an excellent understanding of Agile and Six Sigma methodologies. They have good communication skills to act as a bridge between various stakeholders for smooth orchestration.

Blockchain UX designer: It is important to make the journey of clients and customers as seamless and as enjoyable as possible for quick adoption. This where UI/UX designers play an important role in porting centralized applications to their decentralized versions and create an excellent bridge between enterprises to reflect trust and ease of operation.

Blockchain quality engineer: Adept at penetration, manual and automated testing at all levels of applications, integration, network firewalls and user interfaces to ensure the security of Blockchain system and those of applications and implementation of best in class security standards for compliance.

Blockchain legal consultant: Legal consultants are adept at interpreting existing laws. They understand cryptocurrencies, tokenomics, integrate digital ledger technologies into existing businesses, advise regarding legal implications of Smart Contracts, immutable data and compliance for Government regulations and adherence to ISO standards.

Blockchain network operator: Manages and operates the Blockchain network and is responsible for setting up, connecting peers, databases, local and Cloud environment, firewall and security management.

In most of the large Organizations, the core Blockchain team comprises of Blockchain Practice Leader, Analyst, Solution Architect, Application developers and Client account managers or consultants. The rest of the team members mentioned above are sourced from the common pool of professionals serving the projects across other common enterprise applications. In the case of Consortium and stand-alone Blockchain platform or solution providers, many of the above roles need to be factored in as the operation grows.

Blockchain is an essentially Team-based technology that unites enterprises and various functional domains in an organization apart from Technology. It does not require mastering anything new but reorients one's approach to the new paradigm for a 'Trusted World.'

ANNEXURE: A-TO-Z OF BLOCKCHAIN ECOSYSTEM

Characteristics of a Complete Blockchain Ecosystem

A. Analytics, Artificial Intelligence, Machine Learning for Automation-led future

B. Big data to plan for the explosion of data due to distributed approach and IOE

C. Childlike Curiosity to learn new paradigms as all fields are evolving rapidly

D. Data Analytics to analyze, predict, prescribe actions for the future

E. Enterprise Architecture that balances scale, speed, security, etc.

F. Functional Programming and other advanced programming techniques

G. Game Theory that determines appropriate consensus and reward mechanisms

H. Hashes and Cryptography for pseudonymity, anonymity and Hacker-proof Security.

I. Investment Banking & Economics for Business model articulation

J. JavaScript, Golang, Python, Solidity and other languages to code applications.

K. Knowledge Management to store, update, spread and internalize skills across

L. Long-term thinking and Farsightedness that pre-empts frequent changes and cost overruns

M. Marketing strategies to reach out across the globe in a speedy and convincing manner

N. No/New SQL and Advanced In/Off-memory Database technologies

O. Open-source Technology responsible for rapid adoption of new domains

P. Positivity, Perseverance and Persuasion to envision and formulate a hopeful future

Q. Quantum Computing sensitive approach to plan for future disruption

R. Rapid scanning and adoption of new concepts and technologies

S. Storage and Cloud to accommodate rapid scaling of data storage and processing `

T. Team Spirit, Build multifaceted teams, co-operate instead of competing

U. Unbridled passion to participate in productive and positive disruptions

V. Versatility to be comfortable with Technology and Business Management

W. Wide Networks across domains, Geographies.

X. Xenogogic approach to guide others and be guided in the multifarious domains

Y. Yotta scale thinking to imagine infinite possibilities for the future

Z. Zero-Knowledge Proofs to manage confidentiality and verification at a time

Other Works of Srinivas Mahankali

Blockchain: The Untold Story: 2
by Srinivas Mahankali

Blockchain-The untold story
by Srinivas Mahankali

Secure Chains: Cybersecurity and Blockchain powered Automation (English Edition)
by Abhishek Bhattacharya, Srinivas...

AI & ML - Powering the Agents of Automation
by Srinivas Mahankali, Devaraj P. Iyer, Siddanth Amritesh Srivastava

https://www.amazon.in/s?k=srinivas+mahankali&ref=nb_sb_noss

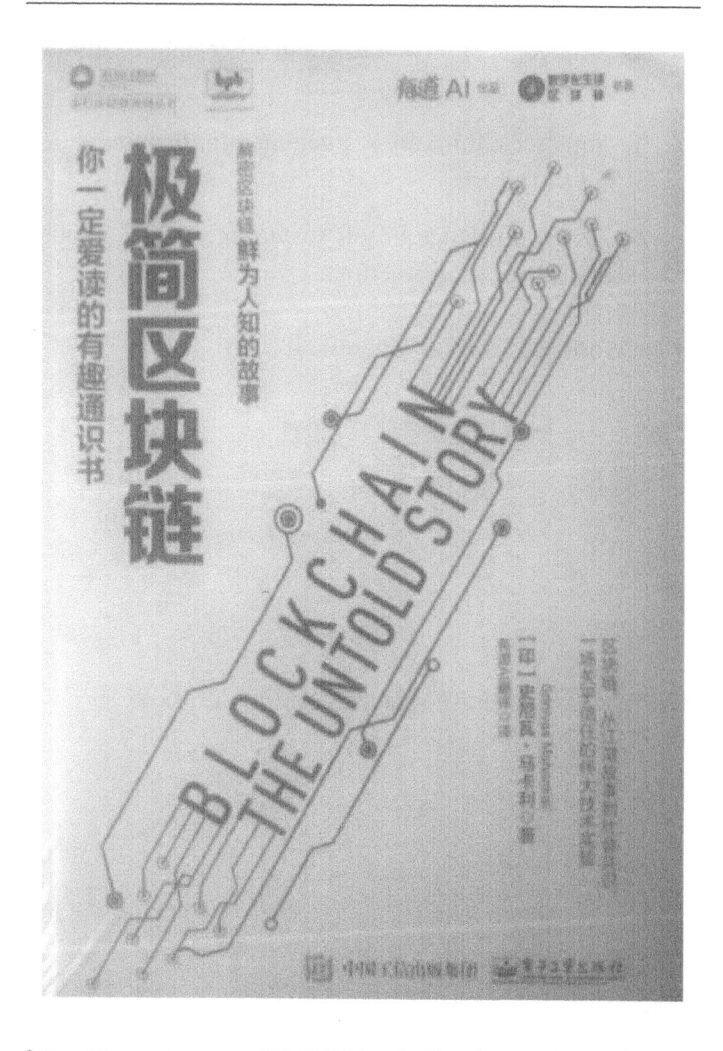

https://yourstory.com/2018/10/entire-book-translates-chinese-30-seconds

https://www.chinadaily.com.cn/a/201809/01/WS5b8a0bbaa310add14f38901b.html